WASHINGTON

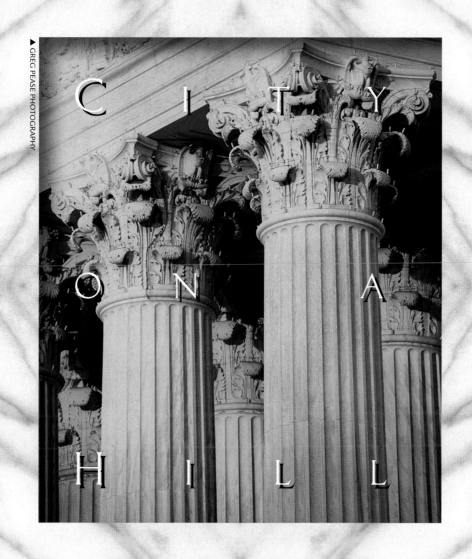

CITY

ON A

HILL

WASHI

By BOB LEVEY *and* STEVE WURSTA

Profiles in Excellence and Captions by NAN SIEMER

Art Direction by BRIAN GROPPE

NGTON

CITY

ON A

HILL

URBAN
TAPESTRY
SERIES
TOWERY
PUBLISHING, INC

LIBRARY OF CONGRESS CATALOGING-IN-PUBLICATION DATA

Levey, Bob, 1945-
    Washington : city on a hill / by Bob Levey and Steve Wursta ;
profiles in excellence and captions by Nan Siemer ; art direction by
Brian Groppe.
        p. cm. — (Urban tapestry series)
    Includes index.
    ISBN 1-881096-41-6 (alk. paper)
    1. Washington (D.C.)—Civilization. 2. Washington (D.C.)-
-Pictorial works. 3. Washington (D.C.)—Economic conditions.
4. Industries—Washington (D.C.) 5. Washington Region-
-Civilization. 6. Washington Region—Pictorial works. I. Wursta,
Steve, 1965- . II. Siemer, Nan, 1957- . III. Title.
IV. Series.
F194.L46 1997
975.3—DC21   97-12602
                                                            CIP

TOWERY PUBLISHING, INC., 1835 UNION AVENUE, MEMPHIS, TN 38104

PUBLISHER: J. Robert Towery
EXECUTIVE PUBLISHER: Jenny McDowell
NATIONAL SALES MANAGER: Stephen Hung
MARKETING DIRECTOR: Carol Culpepper
PROJECT DIRECTORS: Susan Collet-Harris, Nancy Walnes,
Mary Whelan
EXECUTIVE EDITOR: David B. Dawson
MANAGING EDITOR: Michael C. James
SENIOR EDITORS: Lynn Conlee, Carlisle Hacker
PROFILES MANAGER/EDITOR: Mary Jane Adams
EDITORS: Lori Bond, Jana Files
ASSISTANT EDITOR: Jennifer C. Pyron
CONTRIBUTING DESIGNER: Jim Cloud
PROFILE DESIGNERS: Jennifer Baugher, Laurie Lewis,
Ann Ward
TECHNICAL DIRECTOR: William H. Towery
PRODUCTION MANAGER: Brenda Pattat
PRODUCTION ASSISTANTS: Jeff McDonald, Robin McGehee
PRINT COORDINATOR: Beverly Thompson

THE NATION'S MOST IMPORTANT documents, including the U.S. Constitution (OPPOSITE), are housed in the National Archives, which also serves as a library of records and research on genealogy. Here, a researcher combs through a document in the facility's extensive collection, which could fill 250,000 four-drawer filing cabinets (LEFT).

CONTENTS

BY BOB LEVEY

ALL AMERICANS THINK THEY KNOW WASHINGTON, D.C., AND IF PICTURE postcards are the standard by which we judge, then they in fact know the capital city well. We have all been raised on its monuments and memorials, Kennedy graves and cherry blossoms, the majestic Capitol dome and presidents signing proclamations in the Rose Garden. Washington is a city of symbols and facades, of views meant to be timeless and reassuring. To tourists and television viewers, the place might as well be called National Theme Park, U.S.A.

But there is a strong local heartbeat in Washington too, along with a collective case of heavy heart. No city in the United States is quite so elusive or quite so misunderstood. As soon as veteran Washingtonians think they know their hometown, as soon as they think they have it pinned under their thumbs, the city squirts free and redefines itself.

In Philadelphia, there have been Italian parts of town for three wars now, and there probably always will be. In Chicago, most good neighborhoods have been good for more than a century. But in Washington, no neighborhood is the same as it was a generation ago, and many areas of the city bear no resemblance whatsoever to their former selves.

What was once the upwardly mobile, picket-fenced, Jewish-populated suburb of Silver Spring is now a Salvadoran enclave where immigrant families pack apartments, five to a bedroom. What was once the blue-collar port city of Georgetown is now the home of world-class art galleries as well as matrons worth millions of dollars. What was once a center of breweries and warehouses, called Foggy Bottoms because of the industrial odors

WASHINGTON IS A CITY OF monuments and memorials, many of which commemorate political figures and war heroes. The memorial to the 20th president of the United States, James Abram Garfield, is just a stone's throw from the U.S. Capitol. At the opposite end of the National Mall is the Korean War Memorial, which was dedicated in July 1995 to honor those who fought in one of the bloodiest wars of the 20th century.

that emanated, is now a gentrified neighborhood close to downtown, where $300,000 apartments overlooking Rock Creek Park are the rule, not the exception.

Tysons Corner, in nearby Vienna, Virginia, was literally a farmland crossroads when development of the area began in 1970. Today, it is the busiest shopping crossroads on the East Coast and the key job-creation engine for the metropolitan area. As recently as 1960, Prince George's County, Maryland—Washington's neighbor to the east and south—was mostly tobacco farms. Now, it's the fastest-growing county in the eastern half of the United States and home to more upper-middle-class African-Americans than any other jurisdiction in the country.

Arlington County, Virginia, was once a sleepy southern suburb where generals stationed at the Pentagon could find a good game of golf. It is now home to more than 30,000 transplanted Vietnamese and at least that many Central Americans. More than half the children in Arlington's public schools speak a language other than English at home.

In the District of Columbia itself, neighborhoods have withered and wilted, then become reborn in unexpected ways. Adams Morgan, a cluster of tired row houses and modest apartments located two miles north of the White House, was "working-class white" in the 1940s. It became "working-class black" in the 1960s and today is home to a multiethnic mixture of singles, gays, young couples, professionals, laborers, and artists—not to mention the widest mix of nightclubs and restaurants in town.

Capitol Hill was once the land of the political and the childless. Its 14-foot-wide town houses were filled with young aides to old senators. The aides, most of whom were

AMERICA'S HOMETOWN BOASTS a variety of neighborhoods, each with a colorful heritage, exciting entertainment opportunities, and outstanding views. Historic Georgetown, which started out as a modest port city along the Potomac River, has evolved into an area known for its trendy shops and expensive homes (TOP). Capitol Hill is one of Washington's most distinctive communities, boasting such delights as the Eastern Market, with its wide selection of farm fresh meat, fish, fruits, and vegetables (BOTTOM), and the Irish Times, one of a plethora of pubs that populate the Hill (OPPOSITE BOTTOM).

transplanted citizens, almost always returned to their hometowns. Today, Capitol Hill has a broader racial mix than any other neighborhood in the city, and less turnover than most. Instead of layered integration—a white block, then a black block—Capitol Hill is the one place in Washington where blacks routinely live next door to whites. Families have moved in and stayed. Soccer leagues and Boy Scout troops have formed. Bake sales and block parties are commonplace. The Hill no longer lives just for legislation or turns over with each election.

Southwest Washington was once the same sort of backwater as New York City's Lower East Side. The neighborhood's population consisted of peddlers, public servants, and ladies who entertained servicemen in certain time-honored ways. The city's socially prominent residents shunned Southwest Washington, and newspaper reporters wrote sniffishly about the neighborhood's rodent problem. The area was largely bulldozed in the mid- and late 1950s as part of a national experiment with urban renewal. Rebuilt with modern town houses and upscale apartments, Southwest Washington is today home to federal agencies, congresspersons, and corporate executives. The best legitimate theater in the city thrives here, as do fish markets, tour boats, a golf course, and a naval museum.

Amid such variety and variability, is there an accurate window into Washington's soul? If so, what and where is it? What characterizes this city, other than ambition? What unifies it? What excites it? What is the common frame of reference?

The answers are the same to all six questions: the Washington Redskins, the Capital Beltway, and the desire to make positive change. ▶

THREE TIMES SINCE 1972, THE REDSKINS HAVE WON THE SUPER Bowl. In the same time period, they have appeared in the National Football League play-offs 12 times. That statistic, one of the most sustained records of athletic excellence in any sport, stands on its head the old saw about the city that was born in the days when the Washington Senators were the worst team in baseball: "First in war, first in peace, and last in the American League."

The Redskins have shaped social, economic, even religious life in Washington. Woe betide the host who schedules a luncheon on a Sunday when the Skins are playing the Dallas Cowboys. Entire restaurants have stayed in business because they offer brunch-and-ball-game packages. Churches routinely begin their services no later than 9 o'clock on Sunday mornings—time enough for congregants to get home for the opening kickoff.

The Redskins often dwarf so-called important news. One Monday night in the mid-1980s, President Reagan was negotiating an arms control treaty in Iceland with officials of the Soviet Union. At about 2 a.m. East Coast time, when phones began to ring in the newsroom of the *Washington Post*, editors leapt to answer them, figuring that war and peace hung in the balance. Instead, it was a matter of even greater significance. The press corps in Reykjavík wanted to know if Lawrence Taylor of the hated New York Giants had really broken the leg of Washington quarterback Joe Theismann a few hours earlier on ABC's *Monday Night Football*.

Washington has professional teams in every other major sport except baseball. But if you attend professional basketball (Wizards) or hockey (Capitals) games, half the crowd will probably root for the visiting team. At a Redskins game, however, every glimmer of progress brings forth a sea of waving burgundy and gold pennants, and a rhythmic chant of "Let's Go Redskins."

Second-string Redskins players are regularly asked to appear at suburban car dealerships on Saturday afternoons, but first-string Wizards and Capitals almost never are. And Washington lawyers still talk about a notorious divorce settlement in the late 1960s, when a man said his wife could have the house, the cars, the beach cottage, the savings accounts, and all the stocks—as long as he got the family's two seats on the 50-yard line at Robert F. Kennedy Stadium. ▶

WASHINGTONIANS LOVE ALL kinds of sports, but nothing can draw a crowd like a Redskins football game. Fans go to every extreme to show their support for the home team.

W ASHINGTONIANS MAY BE AS PASSIONATE ABOUT THE CAPITAL Beltway as they are about their football team, but whereas the Skins are worshiped, the "interstate noose" is hated and feared. Many commuters avoid it altogether, choosing local roads instead, even though their trip can lengthen by as much as half an hour each way. They simply can't stand the stress caused by the aggressive habits of other Beltway drivers or by the sheer volume of vehicles. Traffic is so tightly packed along the Beltway, even as late as 11 p.m., that a single accident routinely causes three-hour backups. Rush-hour speeds of 25 miles per hour or less are daily occurrences. And everyone has a story of getting a flat tire on the Beltway, parking beside the road, and having no one stop to help for an hour or more.

The Beltway has even given birth to a verb. In the 1970s, when a gentleman named Joseph Nestor was arrested for driving 45 miles per hour in the left lane, he maintained that it was his absolute right to drive that slowly, even if it caused the jackrabbits behind him to gnash their teeth and drop below 75 for a change. Ever since, camping in the fast lane of the Beltway has been known as "nestoring."

"Inside the Beltway" is also part of our language now. The term suggests that Washingtonians are out of touch with the real country (a nickel to anyone who can find it). If you are inside the Beltway, you supposedly eat, sleep, and breathe the prevailing Washington wisdom so relentlessly that you cannot escape it.

In fact, several major government agencies actually lie "outside the Beltway," including the U.S. Geological Survey; the new branch of the National Archives; and major hunks of the U.S. Department of Agriculture and the Department of Health and Human Services. Many others would like to relocate away from crowded, outmoded buildings and downtown Washington parking struggles. Recently, when West Virginia Senator Robert Byrd suggested moving the Central Intelligence Agency to his home state, many Washingtonians smirked at his "homerism." But almost an equal number said they'd support the move if it got a few thousand vehicles off the roads.

A LTHOUGH—IN THEORY—THE Capital Beltway is the fastest route around the city, traffic congestion and accidents all too often turn the infamous highway into a veritable parking lot. Out of desperation, some commuters may opt for an alternate means of travel.

◄ CLIFF OWEN / THE WASHINGTON TIMES

Lobbyists, lawyers, and publicists are still in the loop, however—literally as well as figuratively. They congregate in the office buildings and watering holes of K Street or those of Rosslyn, Virginia (all well inside the Beltway). These well-focused souls, who tend toward red ties or designer dresses, avoid time-wasting pleasantries; a typical opening line over lunch is "So, what do you hear?" They are always looking for their next job, even as they work at their present one.

And after each presidential election, consultants and "image-meisters" for the losing party get together to discuss ways their politicos can recapture the White House (and ways for their own careers to rebound). The next elections may be four years down the road, but in Washington, there's never any time like the present. ▶

OWHERE IS THERE ANOTHER COMMUNITY AS WELL EDUCATED OR AS rich as Washington. The metropolitan area has the highest average household income in the world—not because average salaries are so astronomical, but because so many households have two or more incomes—and a higher percentage of Washington residents hold undergraduate and graduate degrees than in any other city. Likewise, more women in Washington work outside the home, hold executive positions, and earn $50,000-plus a year than anywhere else in the country.

Such wealth and accomplishment have produced their share of excess. More than 20 help-a-mom companies have sprung up in the Washington area since 1990. They take the pressure off the harried and the hollow-eyed (for a fat fee) by bringing in the dry cleaning, doing the grocery shopping, or taking the kids to the dentist. Perhaps equally telling: More families own two cars or more in Washington than anywhere else outside Los Angeles, and more of the cars are foreign-made in Washington than anywhere else.

In other cities, sidewalk vendors sell hot dogs and sodas. But in Washington, many downtown vendors sell espresso. During the record snowstorms of 1996, all

KNOWN FOR ITS FEISTY GOVERN-mental residents, Washington is no stranger to finger-pointing. Three public servants who *never* engage in such activity include Vice President Al Gore and Speaker of the House Newt Gingrich (OPPOSITE), and President Bill Clinton (BOTTOM).

KEN CEDENO

▲ GREG PEASE PHOTOGRAPHY

the major men's clothing stores remained open, just in case some hard charger decided to tramp through two feet of snow to buy a couple of suits.

And yes, the story of a certain eight-year-old is both famous and true. The son of two well-known journalists, he opened his lunch box at school one day and whined, "Oh, no! Quiche again?"

Yet, Washington is a city of purpose. An astounding number of people are here because they are trying to make the country and the world a better place—even though their definitions of that phrase regularly and loudly conflict.

In other cities, money is the measure of success. In Washington, reputation and power count for far more. One wag measures Washington clout in terms of the telephone. As soon as your calls are returned in less than 15 minutes, you're a major player, he says. Fifteen to 30 minutes and you're either a has-been or a gonna-be. More than 30 minutes, you're merely a speck on the windshield of Washington life.

THERE'S A WORLD-CLASS BUSINESS environment in the nation's capital, where numerous international companies have offices. A traditional corporate image remains very important, as evidenced by the reluctance of many Washingtonians to relax their attire despite the growing popularity of "casual day" at the office.

▲ GREG PEASE PHOTOGRAPHY

Yet, for all the pounding pace of Washington, there is contemplation here too, as well as scholarship, beauty, and local history.

The Vietnam Veterans Memorial, which attracts some 207,000 visitors a year, is a place of tears, scowls, smiles, silences, and questions from those too young to remember the war or the turmoil it caused. Elsewhere in town, hurrying is the name of the game. But the Wall is a place where no one feels uncomfortable standing and staring at a name for a few hours.

The main reading room of the Library of Congress is a mecca for graduate students from all over the world. They spread out their laptops and notes and bore in for the long haul. More than 13,600 of them used the main reading room in 1995, and why not? The Library of Congress either has, or can quickly get, every book ever published in the United States.

Despite 3 million visitors a year, the National Zoological Park remains an island of calm and whimsy. Pandas and elephants are the headliners here, but perhaps the real value of the zoo to Washingtonians is the quiet. One psychiatrist took offices on Connecticut Avenue, just across from the zoo's main entrance, so he could walk patients among the birds and wildebeests early in the morning.

The zoo is perhaps more representative of the city than it knows. About 25 years ago, when I lived nearby, a flamingo escaped one Sunday morning. Rather than send

ESTABLISHED IN 1800 WITH $5,000, the Library of Congress is today the largest organization of its kind in the world. With extensive resources and collections, such as the optical laser disc information system (BELOW), the library draws students and other Americans conducting important research.

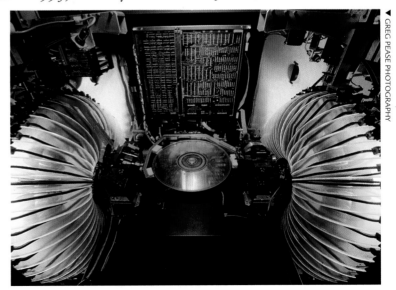

out the marines or a battalion of burly men with nets, zoo officials tried to talk the flamingo back into its cage. Just another job for Washington lobbyists, apparently. (By the way, it worked.)

For beauty, little else compares to Washington's tulips. The first crop was planted under the prodding of Lady Bird Johnson shortly after her husband took office as president. Today, 145,000 tulips and 25,000 daffodils bloom in 70 federally tended flower beds. Flowers may seem like "a lightweight answer in a world of heavyweight questions," Johnson told an interviewer recently. But the world needs "joyful views," she said. Washington evidently agrees, in all the important ways. Only a handful of tulips are stolen each year, according to the National Park Service, even though the beds are not fenced or guarded.

Local commerce is now defined by modern shopping centers, but the old Eastern Market still thrives. Built in 1873 on the edge of Capitol Hill, the market could use some paint and parking, but it still sells produce, meat, and (on weekends) fish to the tune of $2.1 million in gross receipts each year. "Kinky But Ours," says one vendor's sign.

The same sign could hang over Lafayette Square, across the street from the White House, where demonstrators often promote their causes, some for years at a time. Or over East Potomac Park, where rugby and polo games are as much a part of the landscape as softball. Or even over the grain and granola restaurants of Takoma Park, where the 1960s (and refugees from that era) live on. Anyone who thinks of Washington as white-bread predictable has missed the point, or gotten off at the wrong stop.

Even diplomats defy easy characterization. According to the protocol office of the State Department, 12,537 people worked for the 175 area embassies at last count. But they are not isolated and inbred, as diplomats so often are in other world capitals. Spouses of diplomats work as real estate agents, consultants, salespeople at Nordstrom—everyday jobs. Their children attend a wide variety of local public and private schools. Foreign flavor is literally everywhere. A favorite D.C. joke goes: "How can you tell when a regime has fallen somewhere in the world?" The answer: "A new ethnic restaurant opens in Bethesda." ▶

SEEKING INSPIRATION IN THE brilliance of Washington's tulips, the serenity of the Vietnam Veterans Memorial (OPPOSITE TOP), and the motivational words of John F. Kennedy's inaugural address (OPPOSITE BOTTOM), locals find countless ways to improve the world around them, including the annual Earth Day celebration on Capitol Hill.

◀ JOHN SKOWRONSKI / HILLSTROM STOCK PHOTO

◀ MAE SCANLAN / HILLSTROM STOCK PHOTO

W HAT DOES THE FUTURE HOLD FOR WASHINGTON? IF GOVERN-
ment growth slows or stops, the region's economy will probably
slow down too. But that trend might be counterbalanced by retirees,
both civilian and federal, who elect to stay in the neighborhoods and
homes they know and own, rather than move away to warmer states.
Meanwhile, Washington remains the answer to a couple of key questions:
Where else can you find the answer to any question before lunch? And where else can you
live that is equally northern, eastern, and southern?

This is the place where what is national is local, and where what is private is public.
This is the place where you can strike up a conversation with a neighbor about a story in
the news and discover that he or she wrote the treaty or tried the case. This is the place
where you can land downriver at Washington National Airport a million times and still
be stirred by the sight of the Lincoln Memorial just before you touch the runway. Sure,
it is a swamp, in more ways than one. Yet, Washington still bears out the famous stand-
up comedy line: "Where else can so many scoundrels be reborn, and so many non-
scoundrels cheer them on?"

Indeed, Washington is a place where nothing is as simple as the picture postcard on
which it is captured. The more you think you know the city, the more it will reinvent itself. Politicians come and go, neighborhoods rise and fall, and sports teams win and lose,
but one thing will never change: Our hometown will always be America's hometown. ▪

R EMINDERS OF PATRIOTISM AND
pride in the "American Way"
permeate the nation's capital, from
inspirational billboards to victory
parades on Constitution Avenue.

Tremendous local architecture stands as a testament to Washington's ambition.

E VERYWHERE, THERE ARE SYMBOLS and signs of Washington's rise to prominence.

ALTHOUGH SOME PERSPECTIVES belie its magnitude, the Washington Monument is the capital city's tallest landmark, towering 555 feet, five and one-eighth inches above the Mall. Due to a 20-year construction hiatus, the marble and granite obelisk took nearly four decades to build, and a distinct difference in the color of the exterior marks the point at which engineers resumed their work. When it finally opened in the late 1880s, the structure was the tallest in the world.

A LOCAL JOKE GOES: "DID YOU hear the weather forecast? The weatherman says we're expecting a half inch of snow—with drifts up to three-quarters of an inch!" The mere mention of flurries sends hordes of anxious Washingtonians to the grocery store to stock up on essentials, but nothing can beat the peacefulness that follows when the city is coated in white.

LTHOUGH HIS CAREER AS A CITY planner was short lived, Pierre-Charles L'Enfant gets credit for locating the Congress House on Jenkins Hill, which rose amid the wooded flatland that would become the nation's capital. Since then, laws have been drafted and refined on the site for nearly 200 years.

I N THE NATION'S CAPITAL, LAWMAK-
ers and interpreters of the law make
good neighbors. Located directly behind the U.S. Capitol (OPPOSITE), the
Supreme Court building houses the
judicial arm of the federal government (LEFT). The court's nine justices
start each session in early October
and usually release their opinions by
early July.

THE NATIONAL SIGNIFICANCE OF the Supreme Court's decisions is reflected in the majestic building in which they are made. The enormous structure features neoclassical architecture in honor of ancient Greece, the birthplace of democracy. Although there are only 150 seats in the visitors' gallery, the general public may attend open hearings on a first come, first served basis.

ONE OF THE WORLD'S MOST famous addresses, the big house at 1600 Pennsylvania Avenue is home to America's First Family and the site of exciting press conferences and his-toric decisions. The White House draws more than 1.5 million visitors annually, not to mention a regular crowd of reporters who clamor for a look at the action.

THE LINCOLN MEMORIAL IS ONE of the most recognized and visited monuments in the nation's capital. The building, which appears on pennies and $5 bills, has also been the backdrop of many historic assemblies, including Dr. Martin Luther King Jr.'s "I Have a Dream" speech in 1963.

THE MONUMENT TO THE THIRD U.S. president is a tribute to a man who was also an accomplished architect. The dome and front columns of the Jefferson Memorial (TOP AND BOTTOM RIGHT) bear a striking resemblance to the entrance of Monticello, Thomas Jefferson's beloved home in Charlottesville, Virginia.

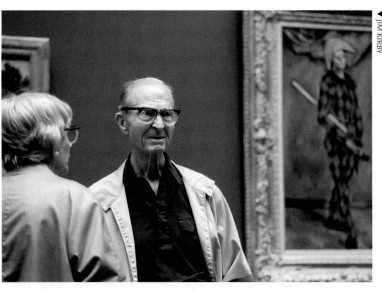

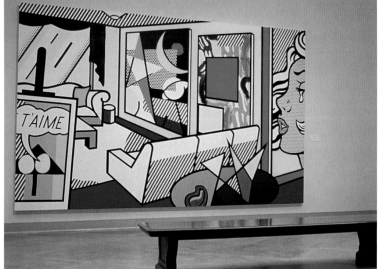

Patrons of all types make their way to Washington's museums and galleries. The National Gallery of Art offers one of the world's foremost collections of Western art (TOP AND BOTTOM LEFT), while the National Portrait Gallery displays some of history's best-known characters (TOP RIGHT). A privately funded museum begun with the works amassed by banker William Wilson Corcoran, the Corcoran Gallery of Art is home to one of the oldest collections of American art in the country (BOTTOM RIGHT).

DEDICATED TO ART

T HE FACADE OF THE RENWICK
Gallery sums up the philosophy
by which many area museums abide.
Once inside, visitors are treated to an

extensive exhibition of American
crafts and decorative arts, as well
as concerts, films, lectures, and
demonstrations.

WASHINGTON

OASTING A COPY OF VIRTUALLY
B every book ever published in the
United States, the Library of Congress
is the world's largest library. Among
its millions of treasures is one of three
existing Gutenberg bibles (circa 1455)
and the world's largest collection of
comic books. Thousands of researchers visit the facility each year to use
its resources, which grow by nearly
400 items every hour.

Tʜᴇ 16 ᴍᴜsᴇᴜᴍs ᴛʜᴀᴛ ᴍᴀᴋᴇ ᴜᴘ the Smithsonian Institution all work toward the same goal: "the increase and diffusion of knowledge." The only museum of its kind in the United States, the National Museum of African Art showcases traditional sub-Saharan African art (ᴛᴏᴘ).

The Hope diamond is the main attraction at the National Museum of Natural History, but the 45.5-carat sparkler is not the only monster on display; the skeleton of a triceratops dinosaur greets visitors as they approach the entrance (ʙᴏᴛᴛᴏᴍ ʟᴇғᴛ).

The Smithsonian Institution Building, better known as the Castle, houses the organization's welcome center and administrative offices, as well as the crypt of benefactor James Smithson (ʙᴏᴛᴛᴏᴍ ʀɪɢʜᴛ).

A STROLL DOWN THE MALL BRINGS a myriad of sights. The Hirshhorn Museum and Sculpture Garden, known for its distinct circular shape, is a mecca for lovers of modern art. Adjacent to the museum are a reflecting pool and terraces that feature some of the world's most acclaimed sculpture (TOP).

Although it only opened in 1993, the U.S. Holocaust Memorial Museum has quickly become one of the most popular tourist destinations in town. A moving tribute to the 6 million Jews who were killed during World War II, the museum traces the chronology of the Jewish plight in Nazi Germany (BOTTOM).

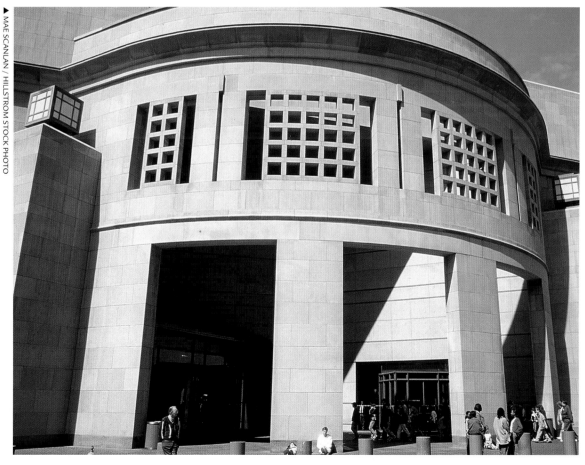

THE CIRCULAR FORM IS CEL-
ebrated in architecture throughout the nation's capital, including the
domes of the Library of Congress
(TOP) and the gold leaf arches that
reach for the ceiling at Union Station
(BOTTOM).

D URING THE PEAK OF THE
tourist season, more than a half-
dozen groups can be tightly gathered
around their guides beneath the grand
dome of the Capitol rotunda. The
tours give visitors an opportunity to
learn as much about the ornate decor
of the building as they do about the
lawmakers and lawmaking of the past
200 years.

S UBTLE CURVES ACCENTUATE
the beauty of Washington's
architecture.

DETAILED ORNAMENTATION AND playful shadows highlight the craftsmanship of local architecture.

Throughout the nation's capital, there are monuments to honorable causes, momentous events, heroes, and even the common man. Often carved in marble or stone, many of the intricately detailed works seem to watch over passersby. A monument to Union Army General George G. Meade at the U.S. Court House (OPPOSITE RIGHT) and one of the many statues at the U.S. Capitol (RIGHT) stand with honor, while *Authority of Law* (OPPOSITE LEFT) and *Contemplation of Justice* (LEFT), both designed by James Earle Fraser, take their place on the steps of the Supreme Court building.

Fraser's *Authority of Law* serves as a reminder of the Supreme Court's imposing power to all who enter the impressive building.

THIS GARGOYLE GUARDS THE entrance to the Cathedral Church of St. Peter and St. Paul, better known as the Washington National Cathedral. Construction on the massive church was completed nearly 100 years after Congress created the Protestant Episcopal Cathedral Foundation in 1893. Today, it is the seat of the Episcopal Diocese of Washington, but opens its doors to worshipers of all denominations.

M EMBERS OF WASHINGTON'S Islamic population celebrate their faith at a local mosque during Ramadan.

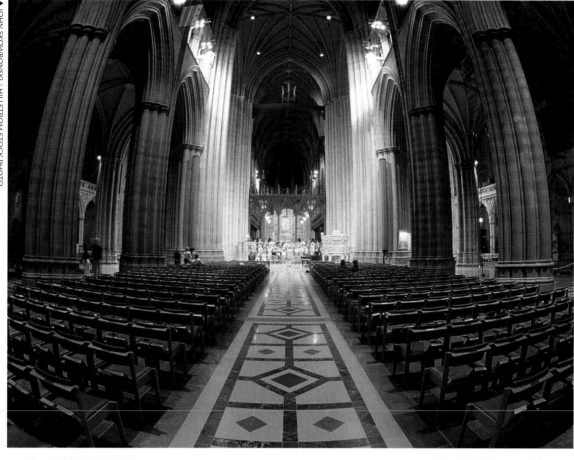

CONSTRUCTED IN THE SHAPE of a cross, the Washington National Cathedral embodies the Gothic style of the 14th century. Visitors to the church are drawn to its magnificent rose windows; the stained glass Space Window, which contains an authentic moon rock; and the Pilgrim's Observation Gallery, which affords a bird's-eye view of the architecture and the surrounding landscape.

More than 5,000 years of Asian art takes center stage in the Arthur M. Sackler Gallery. Part of the Smithsonian Institution, the museum includes important paintings, bronzes, jades, lacquerware, and ceremonial objects from China (RIGHT).

The U.S. Holocaust Memorial Museum, designed by architect James Freed, commemorates those who died or suffered at the hands of the Nazis during World War II. The museum's four floors of exhibits—including videotaped testimonies by survivors, a variety of multimedia programs, and the somber Hall of Remembrance (OPPOSITE)—inspire contemplation among visitors.

THE MASSIVE U.S. PENSION
Building, which stretches 400
feet long and 200 feet wide, is one of
the country's greatest examples of
public architecture (PAGES 62 AND
63). Completed in 1887, the structure
has served as the site of several inaugural balls, including Bill Clinton's
1993 celebration.

THE INTERIOR DECOR OF AREA attractions often is as magnificent as the attractions themselves. The ornate chandelier and detailed paintings of the Small Senate Rotunda in the Capitol give the building a regal appearance (TOP). The Treaty of Ghent, which established final peace with England to end the War of 1812, was signed by James Madison in what is now a Federal-style parlor in the Octagon Museum (BOTTOM). Frank Lloyd Wright called the Corcoran Gallery of Art his favorite building in the nation's capital. The gallery's beautiful furnishings are complemented by an impressive collection of works by such European masters as Degas, Rembrandt, and Renoir (OPPOSITE).

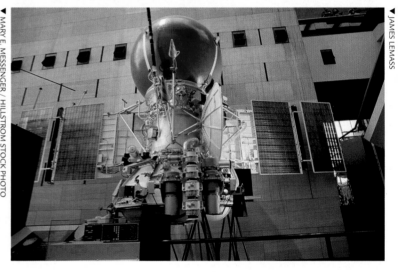

FROM THE WRIGHT BROTHERS TO space exploration, the National Air and Space Museum documents man's successful attempts to defy gravity. One of the Smithsonian Institution's most visited museums, the complex features everything from Charles Lindbergh's *Spirit of St. Louis* to the original model of the USS *Enterprise* from *Star Trek*.

F ROM A STORY-WRITING SESSION at a nearby school to a high-tech mission simulator, computers provide diverse learning experiences no matter your age.

Opened in 1978, the I.M. Pei-designed East Building of the National Gallery of Art is a masterpiece in and of itself. Consisting of two interlocking triangles, the structure houses 20th-century works from such artists as Alexander Calder and Joan Miró.

COVERING MORE THAN 160 ACRES in northwest Washington, the National Zoological Park is home to thousands of animals, ranging from brown bears and camels to rhinoceroses and elephants. For many years, the zoo was best known for Hsing-Hsing and Ling-Ling, a pair of giant pandas given to the United States in 1972 by the People's Republic of China. Although Ling-Ling died in 1992, Hsing-Hsing remains one of the zoo's most popular residents (OPPOSITE).

WASHINGTON

I N STARK CONTRAST WITH THE
daily hustle and bustle, the Mall is
a different world after dark. The maj-
esty of the Capitol and the memorial
to Ulysses S. Grant in front of it is
amplified in the calm reflecting pool.

THE CIVIL WAR CONTINUES TO
be fought around Washington.
Reenactments give history buffs an
opportunity to participate in the
battles that occurred more than a
century ago (PAGES 76 AND 77).

PAGES 76 AND 77: JIM KIRBY

ARCHITECTURAL DETAILS, SUCH as this stone depiction of a ferocious lion (BOTTOM), add power to local historic structures. The ornate friezes of the U.S. Pension Building depict images and scenes from the Civil War. Designed by Army Quartermaster General Montgomery C. Meigs, the structure once housed offices for the 1,500 clerks who processed pension payments for pre-World War I veterans and their families. In 1980, it reopened as the National Building Museum to document and promote the U.S. building trade.

If the Civil War were fought today, would the outcome be any different? Audiences ponder that question as they relive the battles that were fought around the Washington area. Those who participate in historic reenactments take pride in making the entire experience as realistic as possible.

REVOLUTIONARY WAR·1775–1783 ⚓ FRENCH·NAVAL·WAR·1798–1801 ⚓ TRIPOLI·1801–1805 ⚓ N AR

WITH THE NATION'S STRUGGLE for democracy and freedom has come war and honor. From the monuments for those who fought to the grave sites of those who died, reminders of the sacrifices made by U.S. servicemen and -women abound in and around Washington. The Marine Corps War Memorial, better known as the Iwo Jima Memorial, commemorates the U.S. marines who have died defending their country since the corps was founded in 1775 (OPPOSITE). Nearby is Arlington National Cemetery, which holds the graves of more than 215,000 military servants, Medal of Honor recipients, and important government officials (ABOVE).

EVEN WHEN DRAPED IN A BLANKET of snow, area memorials and graveyards exude their power. The 620-acre Arlington National Cemetery is the final resting place for soldiers from the Revolutionary, Civil, Spanish-American, Korean, and Vietnam wars, as well as the War of 1812 and the two world wars (OPPOSITE). Across the Potomac River stand the life-size—and lifelike—statues of the Korean War Memorial (ABOVE). Sculpted by Frank Gaylord, the monument is located in front of the Lincoln Memorial.

▲ GREG PEASE PHOTOGRAPHY

Dedicated in 1982, the Vietnam Veterans Memorial provides calm amid Washington's storm of activity. Nothing else can silence a crowd like the sight of the V-shaped granite wall, etched with the names of nearly 60,000 Americans who were killed during the Vietnam War.

RESPECT FOR THE DEAD IS EVIdent in many of Washington's monuments, including the Second Division Memorial, located in the Ellipse (OPPOSITE, TOP RIGHT), and the Vietnam Veterans Memorial, also known as the Wall (RIGHT AND OPPOSITE, TOP LEFT). Countless personal mementos have been left at the Wall—from teddy bears to love letters to these dog tags, which are now part of an exhibit at the National Museum of American History (OPPOSITE, BOTTOM RIGHT). A sculpture of three heroic soldiers, created by Frederick Hart, stands near the memorial (OPPOSITE, BOTTOM LEFT).

TO OUR DEAD
1917-1919

ONE OF THE MOST VISITED SPOTS at Arlington National Cemetery is the final resting place of John F. Kennedy, who was killed by an assassin's bullet in November 1963. Marked by a slate headstone and an eternal flame, the grave is surrounded by marble inscribed with the former president's inaugural address. The site overlooks the Potomac River and the Washington Monument.

THE TOMB OF THE UNKNOWNS houses the remains of four U.S. servicemen, one each from the two world wars, the Korean War, and the Vietnam War. Crowds of tourists flock to the site to witness the changing of the guard each hour.

Greeting visitors to Rock Creek Park are two 17-foot, bronze statues—*Music and Harvest* and *Aspiration and Literature*—collectively known as *The Arts of Peace*. Designed by James Earle Fraser in 1925, the massive structures were erected in the park in 1951.

W ASHINGTON IS A REFLECTION of a nation built on diversity, and reminders of the country's first inhabitants often intermingle with the city's recognizable landmarks.

Here, members of a Native American color guard march at the Vietnam Veterans Memorial on Veterans Day (BOTTOM).

THRILL SEEKERS DARE TO VIEW Washington from different angles. But federal and district officials have attempted to put the brakes on some of those whose travel habits interfere with pedestrian traffic or threaten to mar the city's structures and walkways.

As the focal point of national democracy, Washington is a logical choice when people want their voices heard. An enthusiastic crowd attended this antiviolence rally, presented in 1995 by the National Organization for Women (TOP), while approximately 1 million supporters of gay and lesbian rights came from all over to participate in 1993's March on Washington (BOTTOM). Though no less powerful in the statement it makes, the NAMES Project AIDS Memorial Quilt inspires quiet contemplation as it honors those who have lost their lives to the devastating disease (OPPOSITE).

ASHINGTON HAS SEEN MORE than its share of protesters over the years. As a group, they are as diverse as the causes they represent.

AFRICAN-AMERICANS HAVE
found numerous ways to
celebrate their heritage, including
dressing in native garb to honor their
roots at the annual African-American
Festival. On October 16, 1995, some
400,000 men attended the Million
Man March, the largest civil rights
demonstration in history. The brainchild of Nation of Islam leader Louis
Farrakhan, the march culminated in
an impressive gathering on the Mall.

BUDDING ARTISTS HAVE PLENTY of blacktop on which to hone their skills. And when they're ready to move on to a canvas that will give them more lasting exposure, there are plenty of buildings that could use a little sprucing up.

Whether you're dancing in the refreshing spray of a fire hose or enjoying a cool treat with friends, there's more than one way to beat the heat in America's hometown.

Washington offers a wide selection of cultural opportunities—from picnicking before an outdoor performance at the 117-acre Wolf Trap Farm Park in Virginia (TOP AND BOTTOM LEFT) to sipping wine during intermission at the John F. Kennedy Center for the Performing Arts (TOP RIGHT). Folks who wish to get into the act themselves also find myriad opportunities to pick up their feet and dance.

PERFORMING WITH JAZZMAN Steve Lacy's renowned band, bassist Jean-Jacques Avenel delights the crowds at the annual D.C. World Jazz Festival, held in early July.

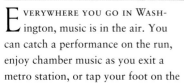

CATCH RESTAURANT
CANAL SQUARE
OPEN
AND DINNER

E VERYWHERE YOU GO IN WASH-
ington, music is in the air. You
can catch a performance on the run,
enjoy chamber music as you exit a
metro station, or tap your foot on the
waterfront in Old Town Alexandria.
Even the Old Post Office sets the
stage to entertain a lunchtime crowd
(TOP RIGHT).

Nowhere else in the country are parades as patriotic as in the nation's capital. Some 400,000 spectators gathered to watch the high kickers and tall walkers make their way along Constitution Avenue during the National Independence Day Parade in 1996.

W HETHER YOU'RE RUSHING TO
work or resting on the green
grass of the Hirshhorn Sculpture Garden, Washington provides for both
the wired and the weary.

BICYCLE RACES NOT ONLY TEST the athletic prowess of participants but also afford outstanding views of the city's sights.

LOCATED JUST OFF THE POTOMAC River, Georgetown University is the oldest Catholic university in the United States. Approximately 12,000 students attend the school, which offers all kinds of educational and recreational opportunities, including a renowned crew team.

WITH PROFESSIONAL AND amateur teams in nearly every sport, Washington is a sportsman's paradise. If basketball's your game, the Bullets will oblige: One-time NBA champions, the team has brought top-notch action to the USAir Arena since it opened in Landover, Maryland, in 1973 (BOTTOM). The Bullets took on a new identity as the Wizards in time for the 1997-1998 season and began play in downtown Washington's MCI Center. Fanaticism for round ball also filters down to college athletics, where the high-scoring George Mason University team packs 'em in at the 10,000-seat Patriot Center (TOP).

AS EVERYONE KNOWS, THE Washington Redskins are as well loved as anything else in the capital city. With a wait for season tickets that can last several years, however, some fans turn their attention to the annual Scottish Games in Alexandria. Begun in 1973, the games offer a wide variety of music, dance, and athletics.

J UST OVER THE DISTRICT LINE in Maryland, Glen Echo Park has experienced several incarnations since it was built in 1891 as a National Chautauqua Assembly. Currently part of the National Park System, Glen Echo is best known for its 70-year tenure as an amusement park, and its old-fashioned Dentzel carousel still lights up the night during the summer months (LEFT AND OPPOSITE BOTTOM). At Christmastime, the new Fashion Centre at Pentagon City offers a festive light show of its own, not to mention more than 100 retail stores to thrill holiday shoppers (OPPOSITE TOP).

THE SHUTTERBUGS ARE ALWAYS out in force in Washington, which provides some of the world's greatest backdrops. Over the years, millions of people have stopped to have their picture snapped in front of the U.S. Capitol.

No one knows it's a dog's
life better than the nation's
politicians.

W HILE THE MALL DRAWS PLENTY
of tourists, locals find their
own ways to commune with the
world-famous landmarks.

CHINATOWN COMPRISES A SMALL section of downtown near the Washington Convention Center. From the Friendship Archway that spans the neighborhood's entrance at Seventh and H streets (OPPOSITE) to a festive Chinese New Year celebration (RIGHT), the community offers an authentic Asian experience.

WASHINGTON

P EOPLE FROM AROUND THE
world monitor when Washington's cherry blossoms will peak so
they can schedule trips to the Tidal
Basin and take in the beauty.

ALTHOUGH WASHINGTON'S cherry blossom display only lasts about a week each year, locals and tourists are greeted with other forms of nature's brilliance year-round.

MAE SCANLAN / HILLSTROM STOCK PHOTO

JOHN SKOWRONSKI / HILLSTROM STOCK PHOTO

FROM THE FALL COLORS OF neighborhood trees to the rich tones of Georgetown's historic row houses, Washington exudes warmth.

Park in the wrong spot during a snowstorm, and you may be there until the next thaw. Snowplow operators clearing the streets often show little concern for the innocent cars they bury.

THE C&O CANAL NATIONAL Historic Park has a little bit of everything for the nature lover. In addition to hiking and biking trails, waterfalls, and cliffs, the park offers a 90-minute ride on the *Canal Clipper*, a mule-drawn barge featuring guides dressed in costumes from the late 19th century.

W ASHINGTON'S RIVERS AND
channels provide the opportunity to enjoy a wide variety of water
sports. All summer long, sailboats
and windsurfers share the water with
larger commercial and pleasure craft.

WASHINGTON PRIDES ITSELF ON its fresh seafood, sold at such open-air venues as the Maine Avenue Fish Market. Located on the Washington Channel, the market offers crab, shrimp, lobster, and other delicacies from the Chesapeake Bay. Even mermaids and mimes get into the act during National Fishing Week.

RON SCHRAMM / HILLSTROM STOCK PHOTO

KAREN BALLARD / THE WASHINGTON TIMES

WASHINGTON

WASHINGTON'S METRORAIL IS A popular alternative to driving. With more than 50 stations, the five-line subway system is one of the finest of its kind, drawing thousands of colorful passengers daily.

Getting from here to there can be a challenge in the nation's capital. Whether it's flying into and out of National Airport, slipping and sliding on an icy sidewalk, or negotiating rush hour traffic, the measure of your success is your mood when you arrive.

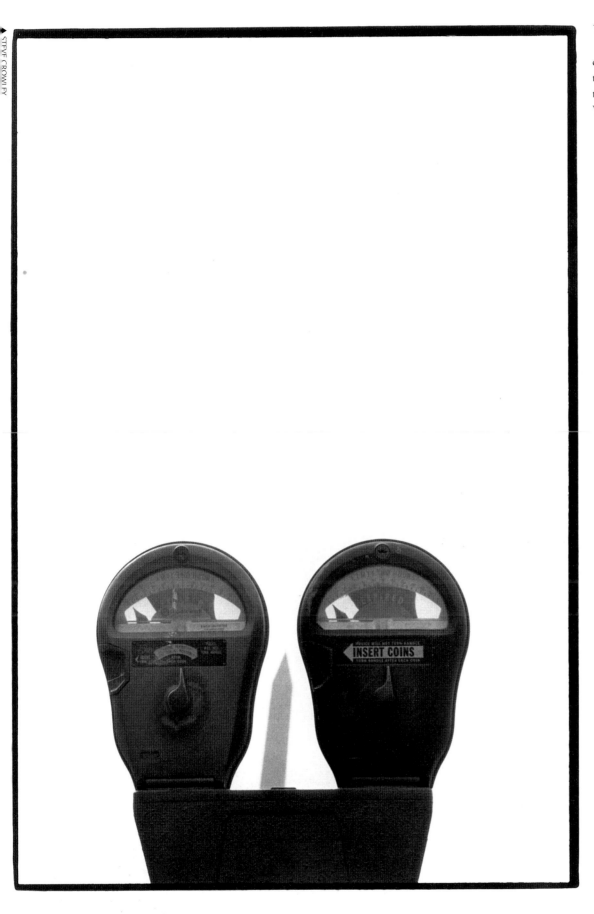

WHEREVER YOU GO, YOU CAN find the center of the nation's capital just by looking up. No structure in the District of Columbia is as tall—or as omnipresent—as the Washington Monument.

INSERT COINS

WASHI

PROFILES IN

A look at the corporations, businesses, professional groups, and community service organizations that have made this book possible. Their stories—offering an informal chronicle of the local business community—are arranged according to the date they were established in the Washington area.

AMERICAN MANAGEMENT SYSTEMS, INC. ✦ ANTIQUE & CONTEMPORARY LEASING AND SALES, INC. ✦ AXENT TECHNOLOGIES, INC. ✦ BEST SOFTWARE, INC. ✦ BOOZ • ALLEN & HAMILTON INC. ✦ CAREY WINSTON/BARRUETA ✦ CLYDE'S RESTAURANT GROUP ✦ COLUMBIA HOSPITAL FOR WOMEN MEDICAL CENTER ✦ THE COMPUCARE COMPANY ✦ COVINGTON & BURLING ✦ M.C. DEAN, INC. ✦ DICKSTEIN SHAPIRO MORIN & OSHINSKY LLP ✦ ELECTRONIC DATA SYSTEMS CORPORATION ✦ EROL'S ✦ EU SERVICES ✦ THE FRED EZRA CO. ✦ FANNIE MAE ✦ FEDDEMAN & COMPANY, P.C. ✦ FEDERAL DATA CORPORATION ✦ GINSBURG, FELDMAN AND BRESS ✦ GRADUATE SCHOOL, USDA ✦

NG'TON

EXCELLENCE

HORIZON DATA CORPORATION ✦ INDUSTRIAL BANK, N.A. ✦ J&H MARSH & McLENNAN, INC. ✦ JERRY'S FORD, INC. ✦ KAISER PERMANENTE ✦ KPMG PEAT MARWICK LLP ✦ LINCOLN SUITES DOWNTOWN ✦ MELLON, NATIONAL CAPITAL AREA ✦ MILLER & CHEVALIER, CHARTERED ✦ NetCom SOLUTIONS INTERNATIONAL, INC. ✦ NORTEL COMMUNICATIONS SYSTEMS, INC. ✦ ONE WASHINGTON CIRCLE HOTEL ✦ ORACLE CORPORATION ✦ RELIABLE INTEGRATION SERVICES, INC. ✦ RELIASTAR EMPLOYER FINANCIAL SERVICES COMPANY ✦ SHERIKON, INC. ✦ BERT SMITH & CO. ✦ SMITHY BRAEDON • ONCOR INTERNATIONAL ✦ SOFTWARE AG ✦ SpaceWorks, INC. ✦ STRAYER COLLEGE ✦ SYLVEST MANAGEMENT SYSTEMS CORPORATION ✦ SYSTEM PLANNING CORPORATION ✦ SYTEL, INC. ✦ TROY SYSTEMS INC. ✦ TRW ✦ UNITEL CORPORATION ✦ VERNER LIIPFERT BERNHARD McPHERSON AND HAND, CHARTERED ✦ WASHINGTON GAS ✦ THE WASHINGTON POST ✦ THE WASHINGTON TIMES ✦ THE WATERGATE HOTEL ✦ WHELAN BARSKY & GRAHAM ✦ WHUR-FM

1848	Washington Gas
1866	Columbia Hospital for Women Medical Center
1877	The Washington Post
1892	Strayer College
1901	TRW
1904	Whelan Barsky & Graham
1908	KPMG Peat Marwick LLP
1919	Covington & Burling
1920	Miller & Chevalier, Chartered
1921	Graduate School, USDA
1930	Smithy Braedon • ONCOR International
1934	Industrial Bank, N.A.
1938	Fannie Mae
1942	Carey Winston/Barrueta
1946	Ginsburg, Feldman and Bress
1948	Booz • Allen & Hamilton Inc.
1948	Bert Smith & Co.
1949	M.C. Dean, Inc.
1956	Dickstein Shapiro Morin & Oshinsky LLP
1960	Verner Liipfert Bernhard McPherson and Hand, Chartered
1963	Clyde's Restaurant Group
1963	Erol's
1965	Lincoln Suites Downtown
1968	The Compucare Company
1968	EU Services
1969	Federal Data Corporation

IN WASHINGTON, 1848 WAS A MONUMENTAL YEAR. THE CORNERSTONE OF the Washington Monument was laid on July 4, and four days later, Washington Gas Light Company was granted its charter by Congress. ◆ Anticipating its sesquicentennial in 1998, the company looks back with pride on its achievements and its contributions to the development of the nation's capital. Washington Gas began as a company with a handful of employees and

one customer: the federal government. Today, it has nearly 800,000 residential and commercial customers, a service area that covers more than 6,500 square miles in three states, and nearly 20,000 miles of gas lines.

ILLUMINATING THE CAPITAL

Washington Gas was founded with the desire of improving the quality of life in the nation's capital. In the early 1800s, residents consistently complained about its muddy, unlit streets and used candles or oil for illumination.

The first successful attempt to use gas in a federal facility occurred when Robert Grant lit a room in the new Treasury Building in 1841. His apparatus, using water-carbureted hydrogen gas

manufactured from the bark of the birch tree, set the stage to bring daylight to the darkness in downtown Washington.

Meanwhile, the successful use of natural gas to light several hotels and buildings at George Town College prompted residents to become increasingly impatient with the oil and candle lamps in their homes and on their streets. Neighboring Baltimore and Philadelphia had gas companies, and Washingtonians wanted a company of their own.

In March 1847, Congress appropriated $17,500 to light the Capitol and its grounds. Just over a year later, a petition was sent to Congress requesting incorporation of Washington Gas Light Company. Days later, a resolution from the Board of Aldermen and the Com-

mon Council of the city was sent, urging Congress to grant the gas company a charter.

The 30th Congress gave its seal of approval to the incorporation of Washington Gas Light Company, and it was signed by President James K. Polk on July 8, 1848. The act created the first natural gas company in the United States chartered by Congress. By the end of the year, the company had mains laid, lampposts and lanterns erected, and the president's house lit.

By 1856, the company had grown to incorporate nearly 1,700 customers, more than 30 miles of gas mains, and about 500 street lights. That same year, one of the first gas cooking stoves in the city was introduced at the National Hotel.

CLOCKWISE FROM TOP LEFT: PATRICK J. MAHER, CHAIRMAN AND CHIEF EXECUTIVE OFFICER

THE AREA'S TOP 25 BUILDERS INSTALL NATURAL GAS IN THEIR LARGE RESIDENTIAL PROJECTS.

JAMES H. DEGRAFFENREIDT, PRESIDENT AND CHIEF OPERATING OFFICER

MARK REGAN

The company survived the Civil War with a little help from a friend. Despite a severe coal shortage and transportation problems, President Abraham Lincoln wrote a letter to the president of the Baltimore and Ohio Railroad explaining the importance of transporting coal to Washington Gas to avert a gas crisis in the nation's capital. The request brought coal to the city, allowing the capital's homes and streets to remain lit.

As the 20th century dawned, the growth continued. Washington Gas expanded into Maryland and Virginia. The year 1934 was the end of an era: the company ceased delivering bills by hand and started mailing customers their gas bills.

The company weathered the fuel shortages of two world wars and the constant changes associated with consistent, sometimes rapid, growth. The company has paid dividends to shareholders for 145 consecutive years, which is one of the longest dividend records for companies listed on the New York Stock Exchange. Washington Gas was always flexible, and it continues a tradition of adapting to change, today more than ever.

DEREGULATION SPURS RENEWAL OF COMMITMENT

Deregulation of the energy industry has ushered in the latest round of change for Washington Gas. In response to the transformation of the industry, the company is redefining its mission and reprioritizing its goals. There is a renewed commitment to customers, which is evident in the company's mission statement: "We will be the customers' choice for energy, profitably offering all products and services at competitive prices."

Unprecedented change in the industry is being embraced as opportunity by Washington Gas. In 1997, the company completed a restructuring effort to continue the

utility's success in an increasingly competitive business environment. The new structure has established three business units. The first, the business development unit, is responsible for the company's sales and marketing efforts, including the development and promotion of new products and services, as well as increasing gas uses and the number of gas customers. The second, the customer services unit, is responsible for appliance service, meter reading, telephone service, billing service, credit dispatch operation, and customer correspondence. Regulatory affairs and pricing are also in this unit. And the third, the delivery services unit, handles all functions related to managing and controlling the flow of natural gas through the system and to customers.

Today, natural gas is the fuel of choice for more than nine out of 10 new home buyers in the Washington metropolitan area. Washington Gas' robust marketing approach enabled it to add 21,400 new customers in 1996 and more than 100,000 new customers since 1992.

As Washington Gas advances, so does its community spirit. The company and its 2,400 employees continue a long tradition of reinvesting in the communities the company serves. In fact, Washington Gas was named 1995 Business of the Year by the District of Columbia Chamber of Com-

COMMON AREAS OF THESE FIVE BUILDINGS WILL BE HEATED BY GAS FROM WASHINGTON GAS. GAS LINE INSTALLATIONS WERE DESIGNED SO THAT EACH OF THE 1,168 UNITS MAY BE CONVERTED EASILY TO GAS HEAT.

FOR THE LAST 17 YEARS OF HIS 20-YEAR CAREER AT WASHINGTON GAS, EVERETT WATKINS, A FORMER RUNNING BACK AT THE DISTRICT OF COLUMBIA'S EASTERN HIGH SCHOOL, HAS COACHED FOOTBALL AND BASKETBALL FOR THE METROPOLITAN POLICE BOYS AND GIRLS CLUBS. "THESE ARE INNER CITY KIDS WHO NEED TO KNOW THEY HAVE CHOICES," SAYS WATKINS, PICTURED WITH, FROM LEFT, WARREN SMITH, GRANDSON DERRELL GRANT, AND TONY HOLBROOK.

CLOCKWISE FROM TOP:
ACCORDING TO BERNADETTE
CUMMINGS, WASHINGTON GAS
DEPARTMENT HEAD OF CUSTOMER
SUPPORT SERVICES, "WE HAVE TO
EARN OUR REPUTATION THOUSANDS
OF TIMES EVERY DAY BY QUICKLY
ANSWERING SERVICE CALLS, BEING
COURTEOUS, RENDERING ACCURATE
BILLS, AND OTHERWISE RESPONDING
TO CUSTOMER AND COMMUNITY
NEEDS. WHEN PEOPLE THINK OF
ENERGY, WE WANT TO BE SURE THEY
THINK OF WASHINGTON GAS."

EMPLOYEES OFTEN WORK WITH
HOME BUILDER REPRESENTATIVES.

EMPLOYEES RUN IN FRONT OF WASH-
INGTON GAS' FIRST CUSTOMER, THE
CAPITOL.

merce in recognition of its good business practices and community involvement.

In 1983, the company organized the Washington Area Fuel Fund (WAFF) to provide a vehicle for the private sector to supplement government funding for energy assistance. The Salvation Army handles the administration of the program, and Washington Gas pays all administrative costs so that every penny donated to WAFF goes to help people in need. Since the program began, nearly $9 million has been disbursed to help people in more than 30,000 cases.

Washington Gas is also a staunch supporter of the Healthy Babies Project, which gives expectant at-risk women access to critical health care. The company is a strong advocate of education, providing materials, scholarships, and funding to area institutions. The company's participation in the Christmas in April project refurbishes homes for elderly, disabled, and low-income families throughout the metropolitan area. These are just a few of the firm's activities that help enhance the quality of life in the Washington region.

THE FUTURE

With a strong foundation of innovative marketing, sharpened customer focus, and five consecutive years of record-setting earnings, Washington Gas is poised to excel in the new era of competitive energy services. The company is testing new markets and exploring and developing new ideas. Customer choice is critical, and Washington Gas is focusing on serving all of its customers' energy needs. This is why selling electricity within the next 12 months is a major goal for the organization.

Washington Gas is looking forward to its industry's continued evolution and stands ready to take advantage of the opportunities offered by the rapid change.

EACH YEAR, SOME 5,000 BABIES ARE BORN AT COLUMBIA HOSPITAL for Women Medical Center, making it the busiest birthing center in Washington. Founded in 1866, Columbia Hospital for Women is today the only women's hospital in the nation with the distinction of being established and chartered by Congress. As a hospital dedicated exclusively to the care of women and newborns, its medical innovation and pioneering new technologies

have benefited women and infants throughout the United States. Although the hospital staff stays abreast of the latest technology, the emphasis is on compassionate care—high touch, as opposed to high tech.

A LEADER IN WOMEN'S HEALTH

Columbia Hospital for Women is a comprehensive, lifetime care facility for women, offering just about every medical service a woman could need. Addressing community health needs, Columbia opened the Betty Ford Comprehensive Breast Center 20 years ago, after the former first lady became one of the first public figures to openly discuss her battle with a disease that has since become a major medical concern.

The Osteoporosis Diagnostic Center, which offers the latest technology to measure bone density in women, is designed to help women who may be at risk of developing osteoporosis. The hospital's Continence Center is the Washington area's first center for the evaluation and treatment of urinary incontinence, and the first such facility operated exclusively for women.

In addition, Columbia operates the Teen Health Center, designed to meet the special health, education, and counseling needs of teenage women. It offers health services ranging from physical exams to screening and treatment for sexually transmitted diseases and family planning services.

Columbia also offers the National Women's Health Resource Center, a not-for-profit member-

ship organization dedicated to improving the health of women throughout the nation. It serves as a national clearinghouse for women's health information, providing women and professionals with the information they need to make informed health decisions.

A HEALTHY, HAPPY START FOR WASHINGTON FAMILIES

Columbia's Birthing Center gives families an opportunity to enjoy all the comforts of home with state-of-the-art birthing rooms that provide a homelike environment for labor and delivery. Columbia also offers an Alternative Birthing Center, designed for families who want a minimal-intervention birthing experience, but providing the peace of mind that only a hospital can.

The Neonatal Intensive Care Nursery provides around-the-clock specialized care for prema-

ture and critically ill infants. This advanced technology qualifies the hospital as a regional center for high-risk obstetrical care. There is a Maternal-Fetal Medicine Program to provide specialized care for women who experience high-risk pregnancies, as well as a Center for Fertility and Reproductive Endocrinology to help parents overcome fertility problems.

Simply put, Columbia Hospital for Women combines excellence in clinical care with compassion, securing women's trust through reliability and a caring bedside manner.

COLUMBIA HOSPITAL FOR WOMEN COMBINES EXCELLENCE IN CLINICAL CARE WITH COMPASSION, SECURING WOMEN'S TRUST THROUGH RELIABILITY AND A CARING BEDSIDE MANNER (TOP).

COLUMBIA HOSPITAL FOR WOMEN IS DEDICATED EXCLUSIVELY TO THE CARE OF WOMEN AND NEWBORNS, AND ITS MEDICAL INNOVATION AND PIONEERING NEW TECHNOLOGIES HAVE BENEFITED WOMEN AND INFANTS THROUGHOUT THE UNITED STATES (BOTTOM).

The *Washington Post* IS NOT ONLY AN INSTITUTION IN THE nation's capital, it's the leading information resource in the region. Most Washingtonians start their day reading stories in *The Post* or hearing excerpts of those stories quoted on local radio and television stations. ♦ Founded 120 years ago as a four-page newspaper that sold for only three cents a copy and had a circulation of 10,000, *The Post*

is now delivered to more than 65 percent of area households. It employs more than 2,500 people and has 25 bureaus around the United States and the world, and a daily circulation of more than 800,000. On Sundays, the circulation jumps to more than 1 million.

A RICH HISTORY

Stilson Hutchins, a Democrat, began publishing *The Washington Post* on December 6, 1877. Three years later, the first Sunday edition was published. From the start, *The Post* was destined for greatness. Early writers include Joseph Pulitzer, who wrote for *The Post* when he temporarily lived in Washington, and Theodore Roosevelt, who contributed a series of Western stories to the newspaper. On June 15, 1889, at an essay awards ceremony on the Mall,

U.S. Marine Band leader John Philip Sousa introduced *The Washington Post March*, written especially for the newspaper. An immediate hit, it is still a marching band favorite today.

In 1905, the newspaper was purchased by *Cincinnati Enquirer* owner John R. McLean, who ran it until his death in 1916. At that time, McLean's son Edward became the publisher and switched the newspaper's allegiance to the Republican Party. As a result of Edward's leadership, circulation dropped, advertising decreased, and *The Post* fell into receivership.

On June 1, 1933, California-born financier Eugene Meyer bought the newspaper at a public auction for $825,000. Though not an experienced newspaperman, Meyer had strong convictions about publishing a newspaper. During the

following decade, the new publisher's enlightened editorial policies and business acumen turned *The Post* around. Circulation tripled to 162,000 and advertising soared from 4 million to 12 million lines. Meyer ran the paper until 1946, when President Harry S Truman appointed him the first president of the World Bank. Meyer's son-in-law Philip L. Graham, who had been assistant publisher, became president and publisher of the newspaper upon Meyer's death in 1959.

During Graham's reign, *The Washington Post* Company purchased *Newsweek* magazine and formed the *Los Angeles Times-Washington Post* News Service in 1962 to syndicate columns, articles, and features appearing in both newspapers. Now with more than 650 domestic and foreign clients, the supplemental news service is one of the largest in the world.

Following Graham's death in 1963, his wife, Katharine, became president of the company, and eight years later, the company went public. Under her leadership, *The Post* formed *The Washington Post* Writers Group to syndicate articles and publish books. Since 1973, Katharine Graham has served as chairman of the board and CEO of *The Washington Post* Company. She is currently chairman of the executive committee of the company.

Donald Graham, Philip's and Katharine's son, was appointed executive vice president and general manager of the newspaper in 1976, and in 1979 he became publisher—a position he still holds today. Donald Graham is also chairman and CEO of the company.

EXECUTIVE EDITOR LEN DOWNIE (LEFT) CONFERS WITH METRO NEWS EDITORS CHUCK BABINGTON (CENTER) AND RICHARD TAPSCOTT (SEATED) IN THE FIFTH-FLOOR NEWS ROOM.

◄ *THE WASHINGTON POST*

Over the years, *The Post* has followed the principles established by Meyer as a guide in producing a quality product for its readers. Those principles demand high quality and fair and truthful reporting accountability to the public rather than to private or special interests; thorough investigation into local, national, and international affairs; and conduct befitting a responsible member of the community.

COMMITMENT TO THE COMMUNITY

The Washington Post's presence in the community is much more than just an information source. Says Donald Graham, "We have a duty to meet the needs of our community not only as a newspaper, but as an actively involved member."

To that end, *The Post* sponsors many communitywide educational programs, including the Agnes Meyer Outstanding Teacher Awards, the Distinguished Educational Leadership Awards, the Eastern High School Incentive Scholarship Program, *The Washington Post* Grants in Education Program, the Grants in the Arts Program, Inside *The Washington Post*, a classroom learning program, and the Learning Partners home-learning program.

In addition, the newspaper sponsors the Suburban Washington Regional Spelling Bee, as well as programs in areas such as health and human services, the arts, youth, and public service.

MAKING NEWS

The Washington Post not only reports news, on occasion it has become the story. On June 18, 1971, *The Post* began publishing excerpts of the so-called Pentagon Papers, which contained allegedly secret information about the Vietnam War. On June 30, the U.S. Supreme Court upheld the right of *The Post* and other newspapers to publish the Pentagon Papers, but not before the

WALLY MCNAMEE / NEWSWEEK

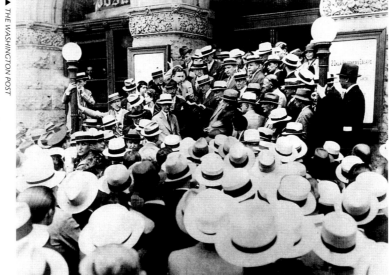

THE WASHINGTON POST

publication became a national controversy.

The following year, *The Post* news staff began its coverage of the Watergate scandals. The dogged dedication of *Post* reporters Bob Woodward and Carl Bernstein is credited with bringing to light the burglary at the Democratic national headquarters in the Watergate office complex, which eventually contributed to the resignation of President Richard M. Nixon.

Such hard-hitting reporting has earned *The Post* worldwide recognition. More than 1,200 awards for excellence have been earned by its news and business staffs since Meyer began rejuvenating the paper in 1933. Those include more than two dozen Pulitzer Prizes, more than a dozen Nieman Fellowships, nearly 400 White House News Photographer's Association awards, and nearly every other award bestowed on journalists and newspapers.

TOP: DONALD GRAHAM, CHAIRMAN OF THE BOARD AND CHIEF EXECUTIVE OFFICER OF *The Washington Post* COMPANY AND PUBLISHER OF *The Washington Post*, IS PICTURED WITH HIS MOTHER, KATHARINE GRAHAM, CHAIRMAN OF THE EXECUTIVE COMMITTEE OF *The Washington Post* COMPANY.

BOTTOM: *The Washington Post* WAS SOLD AT BANKRUPTCY ON THE STEPS OF THE E STREET BUILDING ON JUNE 1, 1933, FOR $825,000.

The strength of Strayer College is—and always has been—its business-oriented curriculum. For more than 100 years, Strayer College has been preparing students to become productive professionals in their careers. Its multiple campuses in the Washington area attract students from across the nation and around the world. ♦ In April 1892, Dr. S. Irving Strayer founded Strayers Business College in Baltimore. He and his partner, Thomas W. Donoho, then started a business school in Washington in 1904. In 1969, the College was licensed to grant the bachelor of science degree and became known as Strayer College. In 1987, the College was authorized to award master's degrees by the Washington, D.C. Education Licensure Commission. Strayer became a subsidiary of Strayer Education, Inc., a publicly held corporation, in 1996.

COMMITTED TO DIVERSITY

According to its mission statement, Strayer College is committed to serving students of diverse ethnic and racial backgrounds who seek a business-oriented education. Strayer offers both full-time and part-time study—at competitive rates—to serve the needs of its students, the majority of whom are working adults pursuing their first college degree.

Strayer College aspires to provide a positive teaching and learning environment. The College seeks to develop its students personally and professionally and strives to build a solid educational foundation conducive to continued growth and lifelong success.

To that end, Strayer provides professional education in accounting, business administration, and computer information systems through its associate's, bachelor's, and master's degree programs. Undergraduate degree programs also are offered in related areas such as economics, marketing, and general studies.

Accredited by the Commission on Higher Education of the Middle States Association of Colleges and Schools, Strayer prides itself as being on the forefront of business trends. The College offers cutting-edge technology courses supported by modern, well-equipped computer laboratories, and, to complement its degree programs, Strayer has a 12-month diploma program in computer information systems.

DEDICATED TO STUDENT SUCCESS

A compelling factor that draws many students to Strayer College is the small classes taught by qualified and experienced faculty who combine years of academic training with professional work experience. The College strives to recruit faculty members who are dedicated, active professionals in their fields, thereby ensuring they bring a practical perspective to the classrooms. Added to these attributes is another key factor: their willingness to assist students in attaining individual goals. In order to accommodate its

CLOCKWISE FROM TOP: RON K. BAILEY, PRESIDENT, STRAYER COLLEGE

THE MAIN CAMPUS OF STRAYER COLLEGE IS LOCATED IN WASHINGTON.

STRAYER CAMPUSES CAN BE FOUND IN NORTHERN VIRGINIA, MARYLAND, AND WASHINGTON. PICTURED IS THE MANASSAS CAMPUS.

PAUL JAFFE

large number of adult students who work while going to school, Strayer offers many evening and weekend classes. In addition, there are classes on-line, which utilize the resources of the Internet, for those who prefer the convenience of learning at home or from an office.

Of the nine Strayer campuses, two are located in the District of Columbia—one downtown and one in the Takoma Park area in northwest Washington—and a third is located in Maryland in Prince George's County. Strayer's six campuses in northern Virginia stretch over an area of nearly 50 miles, from the Potomac River to historic Fredericksburg. The Virginia campuses are located in Alexandria, Arlington, Loudoun, Manassas, Woodbridge, and Fredericksburg. Additionally, Strayer offers many classes and programs at various corporate and federal facilities, making class attendance more convenient for employees.

To ensure that a Strayer education is within most students' financial reach, many tuition assistance programs are available to eligible students. Possible sources of funding include federal grants and loans, private loans, payment plans, and academic scholarships. In addition, Strayer offers a low-interest, no-fee education loan (SEL). This loan program makes it possible for students to obtain an education while making monthly payments.

Strayer offers a wide range of services available to help students and alumni make career decisions. In addition to career fairs and employer recruiting visits, Strayer's Career Development offices provide individual consultations, job referrals, and career counseling. Seminars on job search strategies are held frequently and cover a variety of career topics, ranging from résumé preparation to interviewing and networking. In today's highly competitive job market, Strayer goes the extra mile to help its students and alumni achieve their career goals.

FUTURE GOALS

To serve its students better, Strayer College plans to open more campuses in Maryland and Virginia and to increase the number of corporate and government classroom sites. Additionally, the College seeks to increase the course offerings available on-line through its distance learning program, eventually offering all its degree programs through the Internet.

At Strayer College, the dedication of faculty and staff adds up to a first-rate business education and an opportunity to succeed.

CLOCKWISE FROM TOP LEFT: A COMPELLING FACTOR THAT DRAWS MANY STUDENTS TO STRAYER COLLEGE IS THE SMALL CLASSES TAUGHT BY QUALIFIED AND EXPERIENCED FACULTY.

TO COMPLEMENT ITS DEGREE PROGRAMS, THE COLLEGE HAS A 12-MONTH DIPLOMA PROGRAM IN COMPUTER INFORMATION SYSTEMS.

STRAYER COLLEGE SEEKS TO DEVELOP ITS STUDENTS PERSONALLY AND PROFESSIONALLY, AND STRIVES TO BUILD A SOLID EDUCATIONAL FOUNDATION CONDUCIVE TO CONTINUED GROWTH AND LIFELONG SUCCESS.

F ROM COMPLEX EARTH OBSERVATION SYSTEMS TO DETAILED ANALYSES of fingerprint minutiae, TRW is successfully applying its proven information technology solutions to a broad spectrum of markets worldwide. ◆ Implementing complex information technology solutions requires vision, technological expertise, management skills, and a global approach. TRW's ability to integrate and direct complex technologies has allowed the company to assist

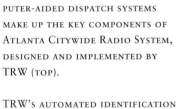

enterprises worldwide as they struggle to manage change in a challenging era of consolidation, downsizing, privatization, and outsourcing.

TRW Systems Integration Group of Fairfax, Virginia, is a leader in the development and application of systems engineering, systems integration, information systems, and software development products and services for government and commercial customers.

RADIO, EMERGENCY 911, AND COM-PUTER-AIDED DISPATCH SYSTEMS MAKE UP THE KEY COMPONENTS OF ATLANTA CITYWIDE RADIO SYSTEM, DESIGNED AND IMPLEMENTED BY TRW (TOP).

TRW'S AUTOMATED IDENTIFICATION TECHNOLOGY IS BEING IMPLEMENTED BY CIVILIAN AND LAW ENFORCEMENT GOVERNMENT AGENCIES IN JAMAICA, THE UNITED KINGDOM, AND THE UNITED STATES (BOTTOM).

DEFENSE

F or more than four decades, TRW has applied its skills to the full range of tactical and strategic challenges of U.S. and international military customers by providing high-quality defense systems. The company's defense capabilities lie within the critical areas of command, control, communications, and intelligence; ballistic missile defense; battlefield surveillance and digitization; mission planning; joint training, simulation, and modeling; testing and evaluation; avionics; directed energy; and space systems.

Over the past several years, TRW has continued to provide superior products and services to the defense industry and transferred its technological expertise to closely related civilian markets worldwide.

SPACE

S ince 1958, TRW has contributed significantly to the major achievements of the U.S. space program by developing both space and ground systems. The company's experience includes critical systems and programs for the National Aeronautics and Space Administration (NASA) and the U.S. Department of Defense. TRW developed the discipline of systems engineering while supporting the air force's Intercontinental Ballistic Missile program for more than four decades as the systems engineering and technical assistance contractor.

TRW is also the prime contractor for the Earth Observing System Data Operations System (EDOS), which provides the first level of ground processing information collected by the Earth Observing System.

ENVIRONMENT AND ENERGY

T RW is leading an integrated government and industry team to help the Department of Energy safely and permanently dispose of the United States' spent nuclear fuel and high-level radioactive waste. The company continues to expand its systems engineering and integration; information resources management; and management and integration services to meet global environmental and energy challenges.

HEALTH CARE

G lobal trends in public health, business, and technology have created a need for better data standardization, improved linkages among databases, accurate data modeling, and improved timeliness and coverage of information products. The best means to achieve a high level of reliability in health care is through integrated information technology. TRW is applying its integration technologies to a wide range of capabilities including image processing and distribution, multimedia storage and processing, video teleconferencing, security identification techniques, and portable workstation devices.

The Centers for Disease Control and Prevention recently awarded a contract to TRW to provide programming and program-related services that will take the agency to the next century. Employing a state-of-the-art client-server system will speed researchers' efforts to collect and disseminate public health information.

INFORMATION SYSTEMS

From engineering tax system modernization and electronic commerce to building financial and banking systems, TRW is well versed in dealing with the complexities of information systems for global commerce. The company's products and services include image systems for processing giros, the dominant payment instrument of northern Europe; client-server open-systems architectures that allow customers' systems to expand as volumes grow; and database systems that facilitate accuracy and security. TRW is also designing and developing systems for processing checks, credit card drafts, remittances, information documents, management information systems, and geographically dispersed wide- and local-area communication networks.

With an infusion of technology and the reorganization of infrastructure, TRW is also helping governments maximize returns and increase productivity. The U.S. Internal Revenue Service is relying on TRW's expertise to support its modernization efforts. TRW is also the prime contractor on the U.S. Treasury Communications System Wide Area Network.

TRW's suite of electronic commerce products and software tools provides a total business solution to meet the information system needs of any organization. Electronic data interchange, rapid text search, software integration, and secure messaging are all standards-based products and services that comprise the company's product set.

PUBLIC SAFETY

Proven systems engineering and integration skills have enabled TRW to successfully apply complex technologies to meet a wide variety of public safety challenges. TRW has designed and implemented integrated command centers and computer-aided dispatch centers, as well as a variety of sophisticated systems for intelligent transportation, radio communication, border control and security, records management, automated identification and verification, voter enumeration, and emergency alerting. TRW is delivering its public safety solutions to international customers in the United Kingdom and Jamaica, and in several localities within the United States, including Arkansas, California, Georgia, Illinois, Indiana, Iowa, Kentucky, Maryland, New York, Ohio, Oregon, and Texas.

SYSTEMS ENGINEERING SERVICES

Developing large, integrated systems is a major undertaking for any organization. With the right systems engineering tools, TRW engineers are able to take on the challenge of shaping the smooth and efficient implementation of complex systems. TRW's sophisticated tools cover a broad spectrum, from innovative virtual reality, modeling, and simulation to comprehensive tools for information engineering, business process reengineering, software engineering, and systems integration.

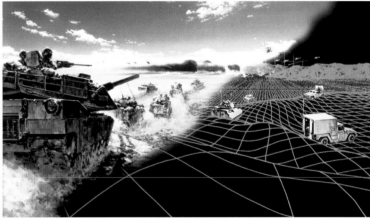

Dedicated TRW teams are working to modernize the nation's air traffic control system through key support contracts with the Federal Aviation Administration in the areas of system architecture, system engineering, automation, advanced automation, weather, communications, program management, and testing and evaluation.

HISTORY

Founded in 1901 in Cleveland, Ohio, TRW is strategically focused on providing products and services with a high-technology or engineering content on automotive, space, defense, and information technology markets worldwide.

A part of the company's dynamic space and defense business segment, TRW Systems Integration Group is a leader in the development and application of systems engineering, systems integration, information systems, and software development products and services for government and commercial customers.

HEADQUARTERED IN FAIRFAX, VIRGINIA, TRW SYSTEMS INTEGRATION GROUP EMPLOYS MORE THAN 9,000 PEOPLE IN 23 STATES AND EIGHT OVERSEAS LOCATIONS (TOP).

TRW IS DELIVERING LEADING-EDGE SYSTEMS FOR THE DIGITAL BATTLEFIELD BY PROVIDING ACCESS TO INFORMATION REGARDING FORCE PROJECTION, RAPID RESPONSE, AND GLOBAL REACH—ALL ESSENTIAL COMPONENTS FOR BATTLEFIELD SUPREMACY (BOTTOM).

WHELAN BARSKY & GRAHAM

W HELAN BARSKY & GRAHAM HAS A VERY RICH HISTORY and can date its origins back to 1904. The present firm is the result of the merger of G.P. Graham & Company and WhelanBarsky & Associates. The firm of G.P. Graham & Company was founded by John Bates, who had a profound and lasting influence on the accounting industry. He was one of three

original authors of the preamble charter Certificate of Incorporation for the American Institute of Certified Public Accountants (AICPA). That document, drafted in 1916, established the professional standards adhered to by AICPA and continues to be the foundation for accounting practices today. WhelanBarsky & Associates was founded by Maurice J. Whelan in 1974. From the beginning, the firm's primary focus was to provide value-added services. There has always been an emphasis on the future. "The past is just a benchmark telling us how things can be done better," Whelan explains. "We want to provide a road map to a better tomorrow."

The synergy created through this combination of history and vision for the future has resulted in expanded capabilities that directly benefit the firm's clients. Whelan Barsky & Graham services the compliance and planning needs

of individuals, partnerships, corporations, nonprofit, and tax-exempt organizations. The firm integrates its accounting expertise with a broad business consulting experience that provides its clients with workable, realistic, and innovative solutions that comprehensively address their business. The

firm continues to provide advice on a wide range of business issues to many different industries. Clients benefit from comprehensive resources, business alliances, and technical capabilities. The firm's state-of-the-art computerized network gives immediate access to critical information about its client base, industry news, trends, and current tax developments.

BEGIN WITH THE END IN MIND

For today's businesses, the world has never been so complicated and uncertain. Businesses and individuals are struggling to take advantage of the same opportunities while planning for an increasingly unpredictable future. The firm understands that it is no longer sufficient to act merely as financial historians; accountants must be progressive thinkers as well. The approach is to develop solid, ongoing relationships to produce insight and perspective on the issues confronting its clients. Each firm member plays a role in designing innovative and creative solutions based on each client's unique needs, providing services that meet or exceed expectations. The payoff is the achievement of the client's business goals and financial success both now and in the future.

CAPABILITIES

Whelan Barsky & Graham offers a wide range of accounting and business consulting services and products. The firm is departmentalized by function. The tax department offers tax compliance and planning for the individual, corporation, part-

CLOCKWISE FROM TOP:
THE OFFICES OF WHELAN BARSKY & GRAHAM ARE LOCATED AT 7700 WISCONSIN AVENUE.

THE PARTNERS AT WHELAN BARSKY & GRAHAM INCLUDE (FROM LEFT) MAURICE J. WHELAN, CPA, MANAGING PARTNER; LARRY D. SPRING, CPA; RICHARD A. BARSKY, CPA; PARTRICK L. PRICE, CPA; LARRY V. THOMAS, CPA; AND DONALD M. COAKLEY JR., CPA (NOT SHOWN).

THE PROFESSIONALS AT WHELAN BARSKY & GRAHAM CONSIDER THEMSELVES TO BE DESIGNERS OF ORDER AND INNOVATIVE ADVOCATES WHO CREATE STRATEGIC ALLIANCES WITH CLIENTS TO ENSURE THEIR SUCCESS.

nership, or trusts and estates, including tax audit representation. Many clients work with the firm's emerging business department by outsourcing their accounting functions or utilizing the controllership support functions available.

The audit department conducts compliance audits as well as compilations, reviews, internal control reviews, and operational audits. Specialties of the department include audits designed to detect fraud or determine the amount of loss where fraud has occurred, and audits performed in accordance with government auditing standards and the Office of Management and Budget.

The firm's ever growing consulting department provides litigation support, including bankruptcy, reorganization, restructuring and workout support, as well as expert witness testimony, forensic accounting, and fraud audits. Additionally, succession planning and change management provides management capability analysis, organizational and process review, reengineering, strategic plans/mission vision, and enhancement of shareholder value.

Some firm members act as mediators during alternative dispute resolutions, perform business valuations, and conduct merger/acquisition assessments. The firm has specialists in the area of estate or gift plans, shareholder options, and buy/sell agreements. The human resource consulting department includes the facilitation of CEO share groups, communication/management seminars, process management evaluations, employee searches, key trait personality testing, management skills evaluations, and comprehensive benefit packages. Clients look to the firm to assist them with business alliance strategies that can include integrated delivery systems, business plans/feasibility studies, strategic operational plan-

ning, cost reduction or profit improvement plans, financial modeling for capital sources, lease/buy analysis, equity versus debt financing, and loan proposals.

CENTER FOR EXCELLENCE

The Whelan Barsky & Graham philosophy of business is driven by the concept that the firm operates as a "Center for Excellence," committed to providing clients quality, accurate, and timely service at a fair cost. Each client relationship is managed by experienced, seasoned professionals and supported by their comprehensive resources, technical capabilities, and industry knowledge. Clients are able to rely on sound, innovative counsel when attempting to solve their most pressing business issues.

QUALITY PROFESSIONALS

The Whelan Barsky & Graham staff consider themselves designers of order and innovative advocates, who create strategic client alliances to ensure success. The firm places special emphasis on the continuing development and education of its staff. This translates into highly productive employees who use their skills to continually research the needs of clients and develop cutting-edge products and services.

Throughout the process, the professionals at Whelan Barsky & Graham "begin with the end in mind." They perceive themselves as extensions of the client's staff, working to thoroughly understand daily operations and long-term objectives. Their task is to help clients identify the critical steps required to improve current financial positions and ensure a successful future.

PROFESSIONAL AFFILIATIONS

The staff of Whelan Barsky & Graham actively participate

in professional organizational activities. They are members of the American Institute of Certified Public Accountants (AICPA), the Greater Washington Society of Certified Public Accountants (GWSCPA), the Maryland Association of Certified Public Accountants (MACPA), and the Virginia Society of Certified Public Accountants (VSCPA). Certain specialists in the firm hold certifications as Fraud Examiners and Business Valuation Specialists, as well as holding positions as board members of local banks and prominent organizations.

Whelan Barsky & Graham is one of the top certified public accounting and business consulting firms in the region because it provides a unique mixture of products and services to address individual client needs. The firm connects its clients' goals with achievements and its clients' visions with reality, charting the future for business and the nation's accounting industry.

THE FIRM INTEGRATES ITS ACCOUNTING EXPERTISE WITH A BROAD BUSINESS CONSULTING EXPERIENCE THAT PROVIDES ITS CLIENTS WITH WORKABLE, REALISTIC, AND INNOVATIVE SOLUTIONS THAT COMPREHENSIVELY ADDRESS THEIR BUSINESS (TOP).

THE FIRM UNDERSTANDS THAT IT IS NO LONGER SUFFICIENT TO ACT MERELY AS FINANCIAL HISTORIANS; ACCOUNTANTS MUST BE PROGRESSIVE THINKERS AS WELL (BOTTOM).

▶ DUPONT PHOTOGRAPHERS

▶ DUPONT PHOTOGRAPHERS

K PMG PEAT MARWICK LLP, THE U.S. MEMBER FIRM OF KPMG International, is a market-focused, professional services solutions provider to thousands of clients from 121 offices across the country. Its international presence is strong as well, with 1,100 offices in 130 countries. KPMG's clients are among the world's most prestigious Fortune 500 companies; colleges and universities; emerging technology firms; manufacturing and retail establishments; financial institutions; and federal, state, and local governments.

KPMG PEAT MARWICK LLP CELEBRATES ITS CENTENNIAL IN 1997.

BELOW FROM LEFT: KPMG SENIOR MANAGER BERNADETTE KOGLER AND PARTNERS REGINA REED, TOM LOUGHLIN, AND FRANK ROSS DISCUSS OFFICE PLANS.

A CLIENT-FOCUSED STRUCTURE

K PMG identifies and addresses the specific needs of each client with its focused structure. It was the first to create cross-functional teams of audit, tax, and consulting professionals who focus on one of five lines of business: financial services; health care and life sciences; information communications and entertainment; manufacturing, retailing, and distribution; and public services.

In addition to providing assurance and tax services, KPMG offers tailored consulting services such as compensation and benefits, corporate transactions, information systems, performance improvement, personal financial planning, risk management, and strategic planning. KPMG's industry-focused structure allows it to position clients in order to help them capitalize on the benefits of a dynamic market.

KPMG AND WASHINGTON: A WINNING COMBINATION

T he firm has enjoyed a presence in the District of Columbia since 1908, and today is located at 2001 M Street, Northwest. KPMG's Washington office serves as the hub of the firm's 3,100-person mid-Atlantic area that encompasses markets from Norfolk to Pittsburgh and east to Philadelphia and Baltimore.

Clients have responded well to the focused structure and teams of professionals in the region. In fact, the Emerson Company's recent client satisfaction survey ranked KPMG first in overall client satisfaction in the Washington area. KPMG appreciates its longevity in a city known for its world leadership, history, and unique character.

SERVICE TO THE COMMUNITY

K PMG's commitment to superior client service is matched by its commitment to serve the local communities in which it conducts business. KPMG people are encouraged to become involved in efforts aimed at giving back to their community.

"It's important that we support institutions within the District, because its health as a city is critical to the metropolitan area's success and as a symbol nationwide," says KPMG Area Managing Partner Frank Ross. "KPMG's business and our people are intrinsically linked to the surrounding community."

KPMG has long supported various cultural organizations, including the Corcoran Gallery, the Smithsonian Institution, the Kennedy Center, and the U.S. Holocaust Memorial Museum. The Washington office displays a wide-ranging collection of original art by District-based artists and sponsors annual efforts to raise funds on behalf of the homeless, Junior Achievement, March of Dimes, The College Fund/UNCF, and United Way.

A CENTURY IN BUSINESS

K PMG's success throughout the 20th century has set the stage for a celebration of its centennial in 1997. Founded in 1897, Marwick, Mitchell & Co. has evolved to become the international firm of Klynveld Peat Marwick Goerdeler (KPMG). Linked by state-of-the-art global information systems and a shared wealth of knowledge, KPMG professionals continue a century-old tradition of predicting and meeting clients' changing needs. KPMG is proud to have a role in helping businesses, not-for-profit organizations, and governments increase their productivity. The firm looks forward to serving as an effective corporate citizen in the District's future. As its centennial motto states, "Our greatest moments are still to come."

SMITHY BRAEDON · ONCOR INTERNATIONAL IS ONE OF THE TOP Washington-area commercial real estate companies, comprised of more than 80 professionals, including 55 aggressive and innovative agents, brokers, and real estate advisers. Founded in 1930, Smithy Braedon · ONCOR International is locally owned and highly regarded as a company stressing teamwork, individual integrity, and creative

hard work on behalf of its clients. The company operates from offices in Fairfax, Virginia; suburban Maryland; and the District of Columbia. Its scope of services includes commercial leasing, tenant representation, investment sales, finance, retail, property management, facility information management, advisory services, and market analysis.

Assisting clients for more than 60 years, the company has established the expertise and the track record to provide real estate services in a marketplace where the flexibility and maneuverability to accommodate client requirements and the fluctuations in the market are essential. Smithy Braedon · ONCOR International approaches each listing assignment with a fresh perspective: first by assembling the best possible project team, and then by developing aggressive marketing strategies, which include detailed financial analysis and projections. The company's expertise allows it to manage complex negotiations involving property owners, investors, landlords, tenants' bureaucratic agencies, or political entities. Smithy Braedon · ONCOR International takes pride in being flexible, responsive, and creative— qualities the company strives to achieve and maintain with every transaction and business relationship.

The results speak for themselves. For example, in the last few years, Smithy Braedon · ONCOR International's leasing professionals negotiated leases representing more than 10 million square feet of space. During the same period, the company negotiated $140 mil-

lion in annual sales transactions alone. A partial listing of both sales and lease transactions includes the National Rifle Association for a 290,000-square-foot building purchase in Fairfax County; Provident Life for 100,000 square feet of leases with Cable and Wireless Communications in Tysons Corner, Virginia; Ogden Corporation for a 137,000-square-foot lease in Oakton, Virginia; COMSAT Corporation's 170,000-square-foot relocation to Bethesda, Maryland; Discovery Communications, Inc. of Bethesda for total lease transaction of 184,000 square feet; Hechinger Company for both a 230,000-square-foot sublease of its headquarters and a 96,000-square-foot lease for its new headquarters in Landover, Maryland; the Motion Picture Association with the leasing of its headquarters at 888 16th Street, Northwest, in Washington; and approximately 500,000 square feet of lease transactions with Hills Department Stores and Pace Membership Warehouse.

Expanding the services and capabilities offered to its clients, Smithy Braedon · ONCOR International recently formed two strategic alliances. ONCOR International Property Services, with Philadelphia partner Jackson-Cross, established in 1994, offers building owners the best, most cost-effective management service program to ensure the bottom line is maximized and that the owner's investment is protected. Coupled with the company's leasing services, the effort is to achieve and maintain 100 percent occupancy through a vigorous, aggressive tenant retention plan. Secondly, a joint ven-

ture relationship was established with national auction company Sheldon Good and Company of Chicago for the disposition of select properties throughout the Greater Washington area.

Smithy Braedon · ONCOR International also offers national and international real estate services through ONCOR International— the client-driven worldwide real estate organization that covers more than 200 markets in 30 countries. With a total of 40 companies maintaining 164 offices, there are more than 2,500 real estate professionals. ONCOR firms generated more than $10 billion in 1994 in commercial real estate transactions, and today manage in excess of 250 million square feet of property.

JAMES L. EICHBERG, CHAIRMAN OF SMITH BRAEDON · ONCOR INTERNATIONAL

MATTOX COMMERCIAL PHOTOGRAPHY

SINCE ITS FOUNDING IN WASHINGTON IN 1919, COVINGTON & BURLING has built a nationwide reputation for providing the highest standard of legal representation and for its dedication to public service. ◆ Covington & Burling's founders foresaw the growth of federal legislation, regulation, and taxation, and sought to create a firm that could advise corporations located anywhere on the broadest range of legal issues.

Since then, Covington & Burling lawyers have been present at the creation of major federal laws, regulatory agencies, and programs, either while serving in government or as advocates on behalf of clients in the actual framing of regulatory standards. The firm's more than 300 lawyers include specialists who can assist businesses with virtually all their legal needs.

The firm's clients range from Washington-area start-up companies to the world's largest multinational corporations, and span every business sector. Covington & Burling consistently ranks among the nation's top two or three law firms in annual surveys of the nation's largest companies, and also works with entrepreneurs in such emerging fields as telecommunications, biotechnology, and medical devices. Other clients include state governments, several foreign nations, and more than 100 trade associations.

DISTINGUISHED SERVICE

Covington & Burling's lawyers are typically high-ranking graduates of the best law schools. Many have advanced degrees in other fields, have served as clerks to justices of the U.S. Supreme Court or other courts, or have taught law or other disciplines. Many continue to devote part of their time to teaching and writing for legal journals or trade publications.

Lawyers currently with the firm have served in senior positions in the White House; the departments of State, Defense, Treasury, Justice, Commerce, Labor, and Transportation; the U.S. Attorney's office; the Food and Drug Administration; the Securities and Exchange Commission; and the Internal Revenue Service, as well as in other governmental agencies and on the staffs of U.S. senators and representatives. Covington & Burling lawyers also work with leading international organizations, serving as members of delegations to the United Nations, assisting the Organization for Economic Cooperation and Development, and participating in diplomatic conferences on international law. Others serve on advisory committees to the National Institutes of Health, the National Academy of Sciences, and similar bodies. Many firm lawyers are deeply involved in public affairs in the District of Columbia and surrounding communities.

CLOCKWISE FROM TOP LEFT: COVINGTON & BURLING HAS ONE OF THE LARGEST LAW FIRM LIBRARIES IN THE UNITED STATES, WHICH INCLUDES FEDERAL LEGISLATIVE HISTORY MATERIALS THAT ARE AVAILABLE NOWHERE ELSE.

COVINGTON & BURLING HAS WON MANY AWARDS FOR PUBLIC SERVICE AND CONSISTENTLY RANKS AT OR NEAR THE TOP IN NATIONAL SURVEYS OF LAW FIRM *pro bono* ACTIVITIES.

THE FIRM'S DOWNTOWN OFFICES ON PENNSYLVANIA AVENUE ARE IN SIGHT OF THE CAPITOL, MONUMENTS, AND THE WHITE HOUSE GROUNDS.

Covington & Burling's commitment to public service also includes representation of the poor and disadvantaged in Washington and elsewhere. The firm has received many awards from local organizations for its *pro bono* work, and Covington & Burling has regularly scored among the top law firms in national rankings of lawyer public service work.

THE FIRM'S AREAS OF PRACTICE

Covington & Burling lawyers represent clients in virtually all areas of law, including antitrust, competition, and trade regulation; banking and financial services; bankruptcy and insolvency; communications; corporate transactions and governance; criminal and enforcement matters; employment and labor; energy and natural resources; environmental; food, drugs, and medical devices; government contracts; health care; insurance coverage; intellectual property; international trade and transactions; legislation; pensions and ERISA; product liability and toxic torts; real estate; securities; taxation; transportation; and trusts and estates.

Covington & Burling's broad experience in litigation and alternative dispute resolution complements every part of the firm's practice. Firm litigators have established a reputation for advocacy of the highest quality and have earned credibility for their absolute probity and civility in dealing with opposing counsel, judges, and juries. They try civil and criminal cases in federal and state courts throughout the nation, appear in administrative proceedings of all sorts, and conduct an extensive appellate practice in state courts, federal appeals courts, and the U.S. Supreme Court. Covington & Burling has long been active in arbitration, including international commercial arbitration

throughout the world. The firm has also been deeply involved in many sorts of alternative dispute resolution, including the design of the pioneering procedures for resolution of asbestos and other mass claims.

The breadth of Covington & Burling's practice also enhances the firm's ability to represent clients in business transactions affected by local, state, federal, and international laws and regulations. The firm has broad experience in mergers, acquisitions, joint ventures, tender offers, leveraged buyouts, financings, asset sales, licensing, real estate transactions, and commercial arrangements of all sorts. Tax, antitrust, environmental, pension, securities, and intellectual property lawyers work as a team in many transactions, along with others whose specialties are relevant to the client's business and objectives.

GLOBALIZATION, INVESTMENT, AND REGULATION

Increasingly, Covington & Burling assists clients in taking advantage of the rapid emergence of global markets. Through its offices in Washington, London, and Brussels, as well as its correspondent office in Paris, the firm's American and European lawyers deploy their experience in trade and investment regulation, corpo-

rate and financial skills, and lessons learned in decades of international representations. The firm helps its clients understand and comply not only with U.S. laws dealing with marketing, product safety, and environmental practices, but also with the growing body of international regulations and standards. The firm works with clients to protect their intellectual property rights on a worldwide scale and to optimize financial returns in light of varying tax regimes and authorities.

Just as Covington & Burling's founders at the dawn of federal government growth sought to create a firm that could advise and represent companies on the full range of their legal needs in the United States, so the firm today is meeting the needs of its clients for legal assistance unlimited by national boundaries.

COVINGTON & BURLING LAWYERS (SEATED ON RIGHT) SERVED AT THE INTERNATIONAL COURT OF JUSTICE IN THE HAGUE DURING PROCEEDINGS BY U.S. COMPANIES AGAINST THE GOVERNMENT OF IRAN. WITH OFFICES IN EUROPE AND CLOSE WORKING RELATIONSHIPS WITH OTHER FIRMS THROUGHOUT THE WORLD, COVINGTON & BURLING ASSISTS ITS CLIENTS WITH THE FULL RANGE OF THEIR LEGAL NEEDS BOTH IN THE UNITED STATES AND ABROAD.

THE NATION'S FIRST LAW FIRM SPECIALIZING IN TAX MATTERS, MILLER & Chevalier, Chartered (M&C) was established in 1920 by Robert Miller and Stuart Chevalier, who brought a wealth of experience to the firm. Miller had served as solicitor and Chevalier as assistant solicitor of the Internal Revenue Service (IRS) shortly after the first federal income tax laws were enacted. Their legacy has carried the firm through nearly 80 successful years.

FOUR PRACTICE AREAS

M&C, which has more than 100 lawyers, has represented roughly half of the nation's 50 largest companies in recent years. The firm assists domestic and international clients in matters involving federal taxation, government contracts, international trade and business, and litigation.

M&C's full-service tax practice emphasizes corporate tax issues. With more than 50 tax attorneys, the practice has earned a reputation as one of the foremost in the country, particularly for handling complex planning matters and large tax controversies. The firm's tax practice is diverse, responding to the increasing complexity of the international tax system and the need for Washington representation to deal effectively with important tax policy issues.

M&C has practiced government contract law for more than 40 years. The firm regularly represents the nation's largest defense contractors, major industries, trade associations, and medium-sized and small companies in procurement matters involving a variety of federal agencies.

The international group at M&C attributes its success to an unusually diverse mix of specialties, a distinguished clientele, talented lawyers committed to excellence, and victories in a number of precedent-setting cases. In just 15 years the group has resolved scores of novel issues, done pioneering work under new legal regimes and before new tribunals, and achieved successes for clients in a number of landmark cases.

Combined in M&C's broad litigation practice are several specialties that usually involve federal tribunals or controversies with the federal government and its administrative or regulatory agencies. Many of the controversies are highly technical, requiring close coordination of experts from various professional disciplines. Industries served include aerospace, automotive, chemical, energy, financial, health care, insurance, lumber, pharmaceutical, retail, telecommunications, utilities, and more.

The firm's strategic plan states: "Miller & Chevalier is, and intends to remain, a firm with a national and international practice in a selected number of specialized areas. In those areas, we strive to maintain a preeminent reputation based on the excellence of the legal services we provide and the

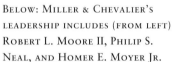

BELOW: MILLER & CHEVALIER'S LEADERSHIP INCLUDES (FROM LEFT) ROBERT L. MOORE II, PHILIP S. NEAL, AND HOMER E. MOYER JR.

effectiveness with which we represent the interests of our clients."

COMMITMENT TO CLIENTS

M&C has a reputation for taking on the federal government in David-versus-Goliath battles on behalf of its clients. M&C's lawyers place a high priority on their clients' interests, and they take pride in their reputation for coming up with creative, innovative strategies for solving their clients' problems.

Philip S. Neal, who has been with M&C since 1959 and has served twice as the managing partner, says he's particularly proud of the firm's long-standing client relationships. "We really work to keep our clients and pass them on to the younger generation of lawyers," Neal says. "We don't want just a satisfied client. We want an enthusiastic client."

GOVERNMENT INSIDERS

M&C has been able to recruit a good number of its lawyers from the federal government. Having a cadre of government insiders, the firm is viewed as a group that helps make the rules, instead of reacting to them.

Larry Gibbs, a former commissioner of the IRS from 1986 to 1989 who joined M&C in 1994, says, "One of the things that drew me to Miller & Chevalier was that about two-thirds of the lawyers have worked in the government at some point in their careers. These folks really *do* know the players at the various agencies. They know why and how things get done, and their insights can give clients and colleagues a real advantage."

UTILIZING TECHNOLOGY

In such a current-events-driven business, M&C has to provide its lawyers and staff with easy access to a wide variety of information. It does that by providing the latest technology and access to all the information needed to successfully prepare and resolve each case.

Robert L. Moore has been at M&C since 1967 and has tried numerous cases before the U.S. Tax Court with record amounts in controversy and thousands of documents to be managed. "Technological support is an essential ingredient to case preparation," he explains, "and we are fortunate in having sophisticated technological support and people to manage that."

Homer E. Moyer, who developed and is the chair of the firm's international group, pledges the firm will remain on the cutting edge of technological advances. "When we litigate cases with complex technical, economic, or legal issues— and little in the way of precedents— we are able to marshal superb resources," he says, "and we intend to maintain that capability."

That spirit of continued excellence has enabled M&C to maintain a tight hold on its niche market. M&C's tradition of keeping up with rule changes in government prepares it for whatever the future brings.

LEFT: ATTORNEYS OF THE FIRM INCLUDE (FROM LEFT) MATTHEW J. BORGER, PATRICIA J. SWEENEY, STEPHANIE P. GILSON, THOMAS W. MAHONEY JR., AND LISA ROBINSON.

I N THE FALL OF 1921, THE U.S. DEPARTMENT OF AGRICULTURE GRADUATE School offered its first classes in eight subjects to 176 students. From those humble beginnings has risen a school that today offers more than 1,500 courses nationwide to thousands of adults. ◆ The Graduate School, USDA is a continuing education institution offering a variety of career-related courses. Although students are primarily employees of local, state, and federal

government, the school is open to anyone over the age of 18. The institution strives to help government organizations—through education, training, and related services—to increase their efficiency, effectiveness, and productivity, in addition to helping individuals improve their job performance and pursue lifelong learning.

GETTING STARTED

In 1920, a joint congressional salary commission criticized the USDA's personnel policies, especially its reluctance to grant leave for graduate training. That document—along with a Bureau of Efficiency statement indicating that many federal employees wanted more education—was the seed that grew to become the Graduate School.

Created in 1921 by Secretary of Agriculture Henry C. Wallace to provide continuing education for research scientists of the Department of Agriculture, the school soon expanded to serve other government personnel.

When participants complete a planned program in some fields of study, they receive certificates of accomplishment. Although the Graduate School does not grant degrees, a number of courses can be transferred for credit at various colleges and universities. Many Graduate School courses have received credit recommendations from the American Council on Education's Program on Noncollegiate Sponsored Instruction.

HERMAN FARRER

A GOVERNMENT ENTITY

A completely self-supporting institution, the Graduate School does not receive any government funding. It operates as a nonprofit government entity that supports itself through tuition fees. The school is governed by a general administration board appointed by the Secretary of Agriculture, and board members are drawn from senior positions in government.

The school employs more than 1,200 part-time faculty who are selected from government, academia, and the private sector. As practitioners of the skills they teach, the faculty members contribute a practical approach to their subject matter to better educate students.

In 1995, the Graduate School experienced tremendous growth when it acquired many training units from the Office of Personnel Management. The acquisitions were part of the Clinton administration's effort to improve the efficiency of government pro-

STUDENTS BENEFIT FROM BOTH INFORMAL AND FORMAL CLASSROOM SETTINGS.

HERMAN FARRER

grams and cut duplicate layers of management.

CHANGING WITH THE TIMES

In many ways, today's Graduate School resembles the school of 1921. It is still an independent body associated with the Department of Agriculture. It is still a self-supporting institution, relying on fees collected from its clients. Its faculty is still composed of part-time working experts. And its philosophy is still based on the belief that adults benefit from working together in formal and informal settings.

Yet, the structure and organization of the school have changed through the years. Originally founded as an institution of advanced scientific study with all instruction occurring after working hours, the school today provides career-related training and continuing education to government employees and the general public during the evening and day and through distance education and self-study.

In 1958, Congress passed the Government Employees Training Act, which required federal departments to provide staff training. As a result of the act, the demand for training in the federal sector exploded. The Graduate School responded by offering special

courses, which were the forerunner to today's daytime open-enrollment programs.

These daytime courses were a complement to the school's already existing correspondence study programs. The Graduate School is a pioneer in distance education. It has offered correspondence courses through the mail since 1939; was among the first to use television and videotape to deliver class instruction; and, today, is a leader in using the Internet, multimedia applications, satellite telecasts, and other technology as vehicles for instruction.

Government employees outside of the Washington area benefit from the Graduate School's nationwide network of regional training centers in Atlanta, Chicago, Dallas, Honolulu, Philadelphia, and San Francisco. Foreign nationals and U.S. citizens benefit from the school's International Institute for Training and Education. And the Career Development Programs unit provides long-term leadership/management training to government employees at all levels. Altogether, the Graduate School offers more than 1,500 courses in supervision, management, and leadership; communications and business skills; personnel management; financial management and auditing; information resources management; program analysis;

acquisitions, grants, and property management; computer applications and programming; and many other subjects.

The nature of the school and its educational methods is continuing to evolve as the Graduate School moves into the 21st century, but the principle that is at the heart of its educational policy undoubtedly will remain the same: government can better serve the public by meeting the educational needs of federal employees. As Wallace put it so eloquently, nearly 80 years ago, "I believe those who may be able to avail themselves of this opportunity will both enrich themselves and enhance the value of the service they render."

STUDENTS PRACTICE CONCEPTS WITH HANDS-ON EXERCISES.

▶ HERMAN FARRER

▶▼ HERMAN FARRER

O N AUGUST 20, 1934, THE INDUSTRIAL BANK OF WASHINGTON (IBW) opened its doors to serve the minority community of the District of Columbia. Founded during the depression, it stands today as a monument to the dream of its founder, Jessie H. Mitchell, and to the foresight, intelligence, and perseverance of its leaders. ◆ IBW, which has always been a family-owned business,

had six employees on its first day of business who took in $192,000 in deposits. The bank grew over the next three decades, and in 1954, B. Doyle Mitchell succeeded his father as president of the bank. In 1955, he became chairman.

Having grown up in the banking community that his grandfather and father helped create, B. Doyle Mitchell Jr. was destined to take over the family business. He worked summers in the bookkeeping department of the bank, and in 1984, he graduated from Rutgers University with a bachelor's degree in economics, with concentrations in finance and accounting. That same year, he started his full-time career at Industrial Bank of Washington,

stepping into the president's position in 1993.

B. Doyle Mitchell Jr. expanded Industrial Bank beyond the District lines when the bank purchased two branches in Prince George's County, Maryland. To accomplish the multijurisdictional expansion, IBW Financial Corporation, a one-bank holding company, was formed in 1995.

When the name of the bank was changed to Industrial Bank, National Association (IBNA) in 1995, the bank's District of Columbia charter became a national bank charter in Maryland, and IBNA became the only African-American commercial bank in the country that operated branches in more than one jurisdiction.

Today, there are more than 150 IBW employees and eight branch offices. In 1996, *Black Enterprise* magazine listed IBW Financial Corporation as the second-largest minority-owned commercial bank and the fourth-largest minority financial institution in the country.

FULL-SERVICE BANKING

For more than 60 years, Industrial Bank has delivered essential banking services that have contributed greatly to the growth and development of the Washington community. Management believes the strength of the bank relies on a prosperous community. To that end, the bank is committed to serving the minority com-

IBW'S ORIGINAL BRANCH WAS LOCATED AT 11TH AND U STREETS, NORTHWEST. TODAY, THE BANK OPERATES EIGHT BRANCHES THROUGHOUT THE WASHINGTON AREA.

munity and providing essential banking services to individuals, businesses, and churches that historically have been neglected by other institutions. The bank currently operates six of its eight branch offices in low- and moderate-income areas.

The wide range of banking services offered by Industrial Bank includes a variety of checking, savings, and investment accounts. There are also various credit services, including credit card, consumer, mortgage, and commercial loans. And for commercial customers, the bank offers deposit account and cash management services.

In order to keep up with the demand for more convenient banking services, Industrial Bank has its own automated teller machines (ATMs) and is part of the MOST, PLUS, and Network Exchange systems. Customers are also able to bank by mail, as well as receive or make payments electronically by using their personal computers. Telephone banking allows customers 24-hour access to deposit account and loan balances, make transfers, and receive other pertinent account information.

CUSTOMER FOCUSED

Industrial Bank always puts customers first, making the community's financial needs the bank's top priority. "Our commitment has grown stronger through the years, and we stand poised to bring our commitment of delivering convenient, personalized, high-quality products to the communities we serve," says B. Doyle Mitchell Jr. "We have an unwavering commitment to uphold the traditions that have contributed to the growth and welfare of the individuals, businesses, and organizations within the Washington metropolitan area," he says.

COMMUNITY COMMITMENT

Industrial Bank has always been involved in the Washington-area community. The bank received high marks for its commitment to the community from a recent evaluation by the Office of the Comptroller of the Currency (OCC), which gave Industrial Bank the highest rating for its record of meeting community credit needs. The OCC "outstanding" rating report took note of the numerous efforts by the bank to interact with and educate the community.

The Small Business Administration has named the bank a "leading small-business lender in the community," and the Greater Washington Urban League has named it the number one minority mortgage lender in the area. At Industrial Bank, such efforts are an essential part of the way the bank does business.

In an attempt to better serve its customers, both personally and in business, Industrial Bank sponsors special programs for community groups, government and civic organizations, schools, and churches. For example, bank employees maintain strong visibility through their volunteer work and outreach efforts. Members of the staff often participate in various workshops, seminars, trade fairs, and school outreach programs throughout the Washington metropolitan area.

The belief at Industrial Bank is that an informed customer is the best customer, and together the bank and its customers help provide a strong foundation for the community. To that end, the bank has sponsored and participated in many seminars for first-time home buyers, consumer credit-counseling workshops, and small business seminars.

The three generations of Mitchell bankers have shared a vision for their community. Today B. Doyle Mitchell Jr. continues that tradition at Industrial Bank with dedication to improving the quality of life of the Greater Washington area.

HAVING GROWN UP IN THE BANKING COMMUNITY THAT HIS GRANDFATHER AND FATHER HELPED CREATE, B. DOYLE MITCHELL JR. WAS DESTINED TO TAKE OVER THE FAMILY BUSINESS.

I N AMERICA, A HOME IS MORE THAN SHELTER, A PIECE OF PROPERTY, OR A source of capital—it's part of our values, a symbol of who we are. For more than half a century, Fannie Mae has helped to make the dream of homeownership a reality for American families by providing financial products and services that increase the availability and the affordability of housing for low-, moderate-, and middle-income Americans. "So much of our identity, so many of our hopes,

are contained in the ambition to own our own homes," says James A. Johnson, Fannie Mae's chairman and CEO. "From the start, a home has been more than another asset for Americans; it has been a motivating idea, a nearly universal goal, the most individual of possessions, and the most shared of American dreams."

UNCOMMON ROLE

Headquartered in Washington, Fannie Mae is the nation's largest private corporation, in terms of assets, and the largest source of residential mortgage funds. "Home" is both Fannie Mae's mission and its business. It's a vital mission. And it's an enormous business. At nearly $4 trillion, single-family mortgages total more than all the bank commercial loans, consumer credit, and corporate bonds in the United States combined.

Whenever lenders around the country lend money for mortgages, they have to replenish their

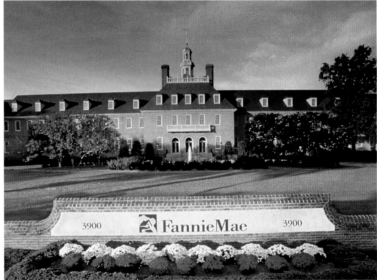

funds from some place. Fannie Mae is where they go. The firm buys mortgages from the lenders, who in turn get fresh funds to lend to more home buyers at affordable rates. In the process, Fannie Mae has become the world's largest owner of single-family American mortgages—one of the most treasured, safest investments anywhere.

Fannie Mae has been helping finance mortgages since 1938, when the organization was created by an act of Congress. In 1968, Fannie Mae became a privately owned and managed corporation, listed on the New York Stock Exchange. By law, the company's business is limited to home mortgages, and Fannie Mae's focus is on mortgages for low-, moderate-, and middle-income families. Fannie Mae now has 10 million mortgages in its book of business, and the average mortgage is less than $80,000. Since 1938, Fannie Mae has served more than 25 million families, and will serve more than 20 million families during the 1990s alone.

That's Fannie Mae's reason for being—to serve people who want their own home, people who deeply believe that homeownership changes the shape of their future and the future of their families.

Consistent with that mission, Fannie Mae launched the Trillion Dollar Commitment in 1994. The

CLOCKWISE FROM TOP: JAMES A. JOHNSON IS CHAIRMAN AND CEO OF FANNIE MAE.

FANNIE MAE'S HOME OFFICE IS LOCATED AT 3900 WISCONSIN AVENUE, NORTHWEST.

WASHINGTON RESIDENTS STEVEN AND ALICIA CARNEY WITH THEIR DAUGHTER CYNTHIA ARE SHOWN HERE IN FRONT OF PARKLANDS MANOR VILLAGE APARTMENTS. FANNIE MAE PROVIDED THE FUNDING TO REHABILITATE NEARLY 900 APARTMENTS IN THIS COMMUNITY.

Trillion Dollar Commitment provides a framework for reaching out to many families who traditionally have been underserved by America's housing finance industry, including people who earn less than the local median income, those living in central cities and rural areas, the elderly, new immigrants, first-time home buyers, and others with special needs. Through this framework, Fannie Mae is working with lenders, nonprofits, mortgage insurers, community groups, state and local housing finance agencies, real estate sales professionals, state and local government, and others to transform the nation's housing finance system by increasing homeownership opportunities for 10 million targeted U.S. families by the year 2000.

WORKING WITH D.C. LEADERS TO INCREASE HOMEOWNERSHIP

As part of the Trillion Dollar Commitment, Fannie Mae has established 25 Partnership Offices, located across the country, to work with local lenders, public officials, housing organizations, nonprofits, and others to help serve residents, especially minorities and new immigrants. The Washington, D.C., Partnership Office works closely with the city and its leaders to develop investment strategies and address local housing needs by increasing homeownership among residents who earn less than the median income; working with the city to improve the energy efficiency of public housing projects; and undertaking special efforts to help finance permanent housing for the homeless and other special needs populations.

Just to illustrate, through one D.C. Partnership Office initiative, Fannie Mae provided $15 million in permanent financing to rehabilitate nearly 900 apartment units in the Anacostia community of Park-

lands. Fannie Mae also joined with the Greater Southeast Healthcare System to help put employees of this community health care facility on the path to homeownership.

IMPROVING THE QUALITY OF LIFE—THE FANNIE MAE FOUNDATION

The Fannie Mae Foundation is a philanthropic organization, distinct and separate from the corporation, yet fully funded by Fannie Mae. The Foundation supports national and local nonprofit organizations dedicated to helping more families afford their own homes, provides aspiring home buyers and immigrants with information on the home-buying process, and conducts housing research. In addition, the Foundation supports organizations dedicated to solving social problems, with a particular emphasis on youth and challenges facing the District of Columbia. "Our commitment to Washington, D.C., is steadfast and will continue to grow in the years to come. As grant makers and volunteers, we take pride that, of all the cities we serve, the greatest variety of programs can be found in Washington, D.C.," says Wendy Sherman, president and chief executive officer, Fannie Mae Foundation.

During 1996, the Fannie Mae Foundation funded more than $4.9 million to 311 nonprofit organizations in Washington—25 percent of the Foundation's total giving that year. In 1990, Fannie Mae launched the We Are Volunteer Employees (WAVE®) program, which is now a vital part of the Foundation. This program is designed to support both Fannie Mae and Fannie Mae Foundation employees who volunteer their time and effort to improving their local communities.

One significant Foundation fund-raising effort is the annual Help the Homeless campaign, which has consistently raised

much-needed money to help the area's homeless. The Foundation joins area businesses in a week-long series of activities—culminating in the 5K Help the Homeless Walkathon—to support the program. In addition to providing financial support, the campaign helps to generate a greater awareness of homelessness and an appreciation for the organizations who combat it. Since its inception, the Help the Homeless campaign has raised more than $3.5 million to aid more than 120 different service providers in the Washington area.

CONTINUING THE FANNIE MAE COMMITMENT

In survey after survey, homeownership consistently ranks as a top personal goal. Americans strongly believe that a home is a positive investment. As American home buyers and their tastes evolve, and the needs of mortgage lenders change, Fannie Mae will lead the way to new and more efficient products, services, and technology to meet those needs. With a global financial reach, national responsibilities, and a community and neighborhood focus, Fannie Mae is committed to homeownership for America's families, a commitment much in evidence in the nation's capital and in communities across America.

AMERICANS HAVE DESCRIBED A DETACHED SINGLE-FAMILY HOME WITH A YARD ON ALL SIDES AS THEIR IDEAL HOME. BUT IN URBAN AREAS LIKE WASHINGTON, HOUSING OPTIONS INCLUDE SINGLE-FAMILY TOWNHOUSES AND DUPLEXES (TOP).

EACH YEAR, FANNIE MAE HELPS THOUSANDS OF FAMILIES IN WASHINGTON BUY HOMES OF THEIR OWN. FANNIE MAE EXPECTS TO SERVE MORE THAN 20 MILLION AMERICAN FAMILIES IN THIS DECADE ALONE (BOTTOM).

A S THE LEADING FULL-SERVICE COMMERCIAL REAL ESTATE FIRM IN the Washington-Baltimore area, Carey Winston/Barrueta plays a vital role in the region's development and economic vitality. The company is regarded as one of the largest and most versatile real estate firms in the mid-Atlantic region, offering a full gamut of services to local, national, and international clients. ◆ Founded in the nation's

capital in 1942 by Carey Winston, the company began as a small mortgage banking and property management firm. Today, it serves a broad base of clients from four regional offices, which are strategically located in downtown Washington, suburban Maryland, northern Virginia, and the Washington/Baltimore Corridor. Total market coverage demonstrates Carey Winston/Barrueta's commitment to serving clients throughout the entire Washington metropolitan region.

Since its founding more than five decades ago, Carey Winston/Barrueta has grown to become one of the largest commercial real estate firms on the East Coast. With more than 16 million square feet of office, industrial, and retail property under its management, Carey Winston/Barrueta is the region's largest third-party fee manager, providing comprehensive services that are unequaled in the industry. The company is known for the depth of services it provides, with client service capabilities that include commercial leasing, property management, investment sales, retail, finance, asset advisory, tenant advisory, government advisory, market research, and consulting and appraisals.

In addition to its core services, Carey Winston/Barrueta remains on the cutting edge of industry trends through its growing subsidiaries: Creative/CW Equities, Carey Winston Realty Advisors, Delta Associates, and Financial and Realty Services L.L.C., a minority-owned venture.

CLIENT COMMITMENT

Carey Winston/Barrueta's success over the years is evidenced by the long-term relationships it has built with its clients, which include the nation's most prominent institutional owners, pension funds, corporations, real estate advisers, and private investors. Growing recognition of its client dedication enabled the firm to double its size during the recession of the early 1990s—and is what will continue to drive the firm into the next century.

Carey Winston/Barrueta is committed to maintaining a consistent standard of excellence in its delivery of services. Senior managers describe themselves as a support team, responsible for providing employees and clients cutting-edge technology, training, market research, and depth of corporate resources. The company's business philosophy and mission are straightforward: To provide ultimate real estate solutions exceeding the expectations of its clients.

CAREY WINSTON/BARRUETA WAS FOUNDED IN THE NATION'S CAPITAL IN 1942 (LEFT).

CAREY WINSTON/BARRUETA IS THE LEADING FULL-SERVICE COMMERCIAL REAL ESTATE FIRM IN THE WASHINGTON-BALTIMORE AREA. PICTURED HERE IS BALTIMORE'S INNER HARBOR (RIGHT).

▲▼ UNIPHOTO, INC.

BERT SMITH & CO.

ALTHOUGH IT STARTED A HALF-CENTURY AGO AS A SMALL PROFESsional services corporation, today Bert Smith & Co. is one of the nation's largest minority-owned certified public accounting (CPA) and management consulting firms. When Bert W. Smith Jr. founded the company in Washington in 1948, his goal was to provide high-quality accounting services to minority accountants.

It didn't take long for Smith to exceed his goals: Today the company employs more than 70 people and maintains offices in Baltimore and Atlanta. In addition, Bert Smith & Co. has become the accountant of choice for state and local governments, colleges and universities, corporations, the health care industry, nonprofit organizations, and individuals.

ACHIEVING EXCELLENT RESULTS

The longevity of Bert Smith & Co. attests to its success. The firm continues its tradition of providing high-quality, reliable service and has achieved a nationwide renown for using the latest auditing and consulting theories and approaches, as well as for its knowledgeable responses to the current regulatory environment. In essence, Bert Smith & Co. is in business to help its clients' businesses grow.

To that end, the company ensures high-quality staffing from the bottom up. The partners of Bert Smith & Co. bring to the firm significant experience in the practices of accounting and auditing, tax, and management consulting. In addition, they are committed to putting their experience and the concept of teamwork into action. The company maintains a philosophy of integrating highly experienced leaders with strategically developed plans in order to meet the needs of clients and achieve excellent results.

Bert Smith & Co. also attracts staff members who have the desirable combination of technical expertise and hands-on experience. The firm is known through-

out the mid-Atlantic region for its exceptionally qualified and conscientious staff and timely service. Employees take pride in their ability to relate effectively to clients' needs in providing a wide range of auditing/accounting, tax, and consulting services.

And clients recognize the difference. They consider Bert Smith & Co. to be a business adviser that is as concerned about their clients' business success as they are.

AN ACTIVE MEMBER OF THE COMMUNITY

Bert Smith & Co. is an active part of the Washington metro-

politan area business community, and its principals are well aware of the factors that contribute to successful business in this region. Partners and staff alike work to sustain the growth and development of the firm's client companies, thereby contributing to the economic health of the community.

Smith was a man who strived for perfection as he looked to the future. Today, his firm carries on that legacy, looking to an ever brighter future while building on a rich heritage.

BERT SMITH & CO. IS ONE OF THE NATION'S LARGEST MINORITY-OWNED CERTIFIED PUBLIC ACCOUNTING (CPA) AND MANAGEMENT CONSULTING FIRMS.

IN A CITY RENOWNED FOR TRANSITION, GINSBURG, FELDMAN AND BRESS HAS remained a steadfast presence in the nation's capital. The firm's attorneys know Washington, and they know how to achieve results. Many have particular expertise dealing with the Federal Communications Commission; the Federal Trade Commission; the National Telecommunications and Information Administration; the Departments of Transportation, Justice, Treasury, and Labor; the Federal

Aviation Administration; the Internal Revenue Service; and the Equal Employment Opportunity Commission. With offices in Washington and northern Virginia, Ginsburg, Feldman and Bress has developed a strong regional, as well as national, practice—working with clients ranging from the world's largest airline to individual entrepreneurs trying to make their ideas fly.

Focus on Business

Ginsburg, Feldman and Bress places special emphasis on understanding the business of its clients. Every client is important. Every problem, large or small, receives full attention. The firm's affiliation with a worldwide network of independent law firms gives clients immediate access to expert legal advice, as well as to businesses, governments, and other contacts around the globe. Its recently formed consulting company, Business Development International, LLC, works on early-stage opportunities with clients in the preparation of business and marketing plans—aiding in the capital formation process—and facilitating corporate strategic alliances.

With the opening of its Tysons Corner, Virginia, office, the firm represents start-up and early stage technology companies in northern Virginia and elsewhere in the metropolitan Washington area, and actively participates in the Northern Virginia Technology Council.

Value in Service

When David Ginsburg put out his shingle in 1946, he knew how he wanted to serve his clients: "Use legal know-how to provide timely service at acceptable costs. Help clients make rational decisions and understand the legal consequences of what they want to achieve. Recruit the best lawyers and help them develop into well-rounded practitioners. Offer expertise and maturity."

Times have changed. But the need for value in legal services is more critical now than ever. Ginsburg, Feldman and Bress strikes the right balance in solv-

ing clients' problems through the efficient and targeted application of its lawyers' expertise. Cost consciousness is not a habit recently acquired—it is a principle that has been practiced since the firm's founding. Cases are staffed appropriately, and clients are kept informed and maintain control of their legal budgets.

Expertise

Ginsburg, Feldman and Bress' attorneys practice in a number of areas. In the aviation industry, the firm's regular clients include major and national airlines, regional carriers, an all-cargo carrier, as well as certain foreign air carriers and an aircraft leasing company. It regularly represents clients in substantially all aspects of aircraft financing and lease transactions and in tax negotiations and counseling in connection with aircraft lease and finance transactions. The aviation practice covers a variety of other matters involving aircraft acquisitions and sales, agency and court litigation, taxation, and legislative and regulatory issues aris-

"GINSBURG, FELDMAN AND BRESS IS A FIRST-RATE LAW FIRM," SAYS THE CEO OF A MULTIMILLION-DOLLAR COMPUTER COMPANY. "EVERY LEGAL MATTER WE REFER TO THEM IS HANDLED EFFICIENTLY AND COST EFFECTIVELY BY EXPERTS WHO KNOW HOW BUSINESSPEOPLE THINK."

STOCK ILLUSTRATION SOURCE

STOCK ILLUSTRATION SOURCE

ing before federal, state, and local governmental agencies.

The firm's business practice group includes corporate, securities, real estate, trademark, loan documentation and workout, and antitrust practitioners. They serve as corporate and securities counsel for several public compa-

nies, and represent many private corporations nationally and internationally. The group is active in representing start-up and early stage technology companies. They are consulted, for example, with respect to mergers, stock and asset acquisitions, debt and equity financing, corporate restructurings, and leveraged buyouts. For many of its smaller and midmarket corporate clients, the firm serves as general counsel, advising on a variety of employment problems, licensing agreements, and other issues. The firm's real estate practice includes a subsidiary title company, Presidential Title, Inc. Antitrust matters, such as Hart-Scott-Rodino filings, are routine for the experienced attorneys in this area.

Ginsburg, Feldman and Bress has special expertise in telecommunications law, policy, technology, finance, and economics. The firm's communications attorneys are recognized experts, including a former commissioner of the Federal Communications Commission, a former assistant secretary of

commerce for communications and information (the highest ranking communications policy position in the executive branch of the federal government), and other experts in the fields of common carrier, broadcast, wireless, on-line, and interactive services.

The firm's employment lawyers handle matters involving the wage and hour laws, employment taxes, employee terminations, employee privacy, employment handbooks, contracts, post-employment restrictive covenants, ERISA and other pension matters, nonpension federal benefits, immigration, and equal employment opportunity. The attorneys have participated in the drafting, implementation, and enforcement of many federal employment laws and regulations; in negotiating with key officials from the White House, the departments of Justice and Labor, Internal Revenue Service, and other agencies to resolve disputes; and in testifying before Congressional committees on tax, labor, and small business issues.

Ginsburg, Feldman and Bress' litigation practice includes civil and commercial litigation, white collar crime, and bankruptcy and creditors' rights. The firm has worked closely with (and against) the Department of Justice in matters ranging from antitrust to the Foreign Corrupt Practices Act, has represented clients called to testify before Congressional committees, or with matters in dispute at the State Department, Department of Commerce, and before the Securities and Exchange Commission, as well as before international tribunals. Its practice also emphasizes alternative dispute resolution as an efficient and cost-effective means of client representation.

The firm's tax practitioners represent clients in all aspects of federal income, estate, and gift

taxation, including corporate, real estate, partnership, employee benefits, estate tax, and nonprofit organization tax matters. This practice is especially well known for its representation of nonprofit entities in the acquisition and sale of affordable housing and with respect to transactions involving multilayered financing and the coordination of resources from tax credits, syndications, participation loans from conventional lenders, state and local government grants, and nonprofit foundation grants.

Neither a megafirm nor a law boutique, Ginsburg, Feldman and Bress' 70 lawyers get to the bottom of the most sophisticated legal issues, recognize when a matter is simple and handle it simply, achieve results without extravagance, and provide the exact services clients need to succeed—no more, no less.

"WHAT IMPRESSES ME MOST ABOUT GINSBURG, FELDMAN AND BRESS IS ITS RESPONSIVENESS," SAYS THE PRESIDENT OF A WEST COAST TELE-COMMUNICATIONS COMPANY. "WHEN I NEED HELP, THE FIRM RESPONDS RIGHT AWAY. THIS APPLIES NOT ONLY TO URGENT MATTERS BUT TO ROUTINE ONES AS WELL."

Booz · Allen & Hamilton Inc.

O NE OF THE WORLD'S LARGEST CONSULTING FIRMS, BOOZ · ALLEN & Hamilton Inc. is an international management and technology consulting firm that is committed to helping senior management solve complex problems. Booz · Allen provides services in strategy, systems, operations, and technology to clients throughout the world. ◆ Although it was founded in 1914 in Chicago,

Booz · Allen owes a major debt to this region. It is one of the Washington, D.C., area's largest companies, with nearly half of its business attributed to the region's largest employer: the federal government. In addition, more than one-third of the firm's worldwide staff of 7,000 are based in the Washington area, and its corporate headquarters is located in McLean, Virginia.

Booz · Allen's clients include most of the largest industrial and service corporations in the world, all major departments and agencies of the federal government, and major institutions and government bodies around the world. The firm has offices on six continents.

WORLDWIDE TECHNOLOGY BUSINESS

O f Booz · Allen's two major units, the Worldwide Technology Business is based in McLean. Federal government agencies are its primary clients, and much of its business is handled in this region. The vision is: "To be the absolute best management and technology consulting firm, measured by the value we deliver to clients and by our spirit of partnership."

Reflecting the explosion in technological advances in recent years, the Worldwide Technology Business focuses on technology, engineering, and management services; systems development/ systems integration in the areas of defense weapon and command, control, and communications (C3) systems; telecommunications; civilian systems; environment and energy; transportation and space; intelligence systems; and international projects. The unit strives to make its client's mission its own; to meet the client's needs from mission definition through operations support; and to couple superior understanding of the client's environment with outstanding functional expertise in management, technology, and engineering disciplines.

WORLDWIDE COMMERCIAL BUSINESS

B ased in New York City, Booz · Allen's Worldwide Commercial Business focuses on renewal, productivity improvement, innovation, growth management, and business restructuring for industrial and service corporations. The Worldwide Commercial Business is organized along industry-focused professional communities in the areas of consumer products; retailing and media; financial services; engineering and manufacturing; energy, chemicals, and pharmaceuticals; and communications, computing, and electronics. Clients of Booz · Allen's Worldwide Commercial Business are the largest industrial and service corporations in the world.

TEAM SPIRIT

B ooz · Allen's team-based structure fosters a spirit of cooperation and collegiality among its staff. On joining Booz · Allen, staff members are assigned to both a home team focused on one of the firm's primary market areas and to a project team, where they perform work on specific contracts and participate in new business development. As staff members gain expertise and learn the business, they begin managing tasks

BOOZ · ALLEN PROVIDES SERVICES IN STRATEGY, SYSTEMS, OPERATIONS, AND TECHNOLOGY TO CLIENTS THROUGHOUT THE WORLD (TOP).

WHAT DISTINGUISHES BOOZ · ALLEN'S COMMUNITY RELATIONS PROGRAM IS THE DIRECT LINK BETWEEN ACTIVE EMPLOYEE PARTICIPATION AND THE FIRM'S SUPPORT OF VOLUNTEER AND COMMUNITY SERVICE ACTIVITIES (BOTTOM).

and proposal efforts, and eventually whole programs for their team.

Success at Booz·Allen is measured by the team's performance in delivering outstanding value to clients, and staff members are rewarded individually for their contribution to that success. The firm looks for people with imagination, technical expertise, and leadership ability. It offers them opportunities to grow and recognizes their achievement with greater levels of responsibility and further advancement opportunities.

Booz·Allen takes great pride in its reputation for excellence and the high quality of its diverse workforce. The firm is committed to broadening that diversity and to providing its staff a rich environment for professional growth. From their first day at Booz·Allen, staff are challenged by work that calls on their creativity and insight and enhances their technical and management skills. Formal training begins with a multiday orientation program and continues

with in-house training programs, a tuition assistance program, and opportunities for participation in professional conferences and seminars. Many project teams also work together on "cross team" assignments and proposals, providing their staff further opportunities to gain new expertise and exposure within the firm.

COMMUNITY RELATIONS PROGRAM

Booz·Allen understands that good business and good citizenship go hand in hand. In the early 1990s, the firm created a formal Community Relations Program to encourage volunteerism and place the firm's assets behind staff involvement in the community. The goal is to build relationships within the community, thereby building opportunities for both business and staff development.

The Community Relations Program encourages corporate support to organizations and activities in which Booz·Allen employees have a significant personal involvement, uses the

firm's resources to further the well-being of employees and support their own charitable giving and volunteer activity, and applies the same professionalism and creative management processes that characterize Booz·Allen's other activities.

What distinguishes Booz·Allen's Community Relations Program is the direct link between active employee participation and the firm's support of volunteer or community service activities. The firm and its staff are involved in more than 100 activities in the areas of education, health and welfare, and culture and the arts. Through the program, the firm and its employees also support many civic organizations.

Booz·Allen's commitment to supporting the communities in which it serves mirrors the effort the firm demonstrates when serving its clients. Today Booz·Allen is working closely with the world's major corporations and institutions to reshape and lead their industries into the 21st century.

REFLECTING THE EXPLOSION IN TECHNOLOGICAL ADVANCES IN RECENT YEARS, THE WORLDWIDE TECHNOLOGY BUSINESS FOCUSES ON TECHNOLOGY, ENGINEERING, AND MANAGEMENT SERVICES; SYSTEMS DEVELOPMENT/SYSTEMS INTEGRATION IN THE AREAS OF DEFENSE WEAPON AND C3 SYSTEMS; TELECOMMUNICATIONS; CIVILIAN SYSTEMS; ENVIRONMENT AND ENERGY; TRANSPORTATION AND SPACE; INTELLIGENCE SYSTEMS; AND INTERNATIONAL PROJECTS.

M.C. DEAN, INC.

STABLISHED IN 1949, M.C. DEAN, INC. HAS NEARLY A HALF CENTURY of proven success in the installation, renovation, and maintenance of all classes of communications, electronics, and electrical systems. The company was founded by M.C. Dean, an electrician who became a civilian contractor after leaving the navy at the end of World War II. Today, the firm employs more than 300 outstanding journeymen, project managers, engineers, estimators, and support staff. This group enables the company to excel in a comprehensive array of services for projects ranging in size from 1,000 to 200,000 hours of in-house labor, with dollar values from $25,000 to more than $12 million.

TECHNICAL EXCELLENCE

M.C. Dean, Inc., which has been managed by professional engineers since 1974, takes pride in the fact that the company has successfully completed more than

ERIC TAYLOR

ALL PROJECTS, EQUIPMENT, CORPORATE RESOURCES, AND PERSONNEL ARE HANDLED FROM M.C. DEAN, INC.-OWNED HEADQUARTERS IN SCENIC NORTHERN VIRGINIA (LEFT).

M.C. DEAN, INC. HAS UNDERTAKEN HUNDREDS OF TECHNICALLY COMPLEX PROJECTS IN NUMEROUS FACILITIES WITH HISTORICALLY SIGNIFICANT BUILDINGS AND GROUNDS LOCATED IN DOWNTOWN WASHINGTON AND THE SURROUNDING METROPOLITAN AREA (RIGHT).

3,000 major projects, all on time and many ahead of schedule. William Dean, vice president and grandson of the company's founder, says, "We've always had a philosophy of doing the most challenging work. Not just doing the biggest, most well-known projects, but doing the projects that have the most technical complexity."

Through the years, M.C. Dean, Inc. has earned a reputation for technical excellence. The company's position as an innovator has been demonstrated by its early proficiency in advanced system technologies

such as fiber optics and complex electronic systems. These abilities, coupled with the company's skill in construction and contracting practices, provide the company with the flexibility and imagination needed to meet the individual needs of its clients.

"Wherever agencies and customers need us to be, we will go that way," says Casey Dean, president and chief executive officer. "We will take on that responsibility. We'll educate the proper people and learn how to do what we have to do."

CORPORATE STRUCTURE

M.C. Dean, Inc. marries technology with construction. "Our primary focus is on the technical end of specialty construction and systems integration," says William Dean. "I like to say that we have one foot in the construction industry and one foot in systems integration. This company is one of the most advanced in bringing those two industries together."

The mainstay of the company's business throughout its history has been its power and energy division. As one of the most capable industrial electrical construction companies in the mid-Atlantic region, M.C. Dean, Inc. boasts vast experience in the construction, maintenance, and commissioning of complex power distribution systems, including primary distribution, motor controls, secondary systems, and lighting.

The communications systems division includes the areas of fiber optics; voice, video, and data networks; and antenna systems. It has been a growing force in the company since the early 1970s. Today, it is one of the premier firms in the region in this discipline, with expertise that includes large-scale integrated voice and data networks, computer telephony integration, complex video systems, and sophisticated command, control, and communications applications.

M.C. Dean, Inc. has also been a prime contractor over the past 30 years in advanced facility electronic systems such as security, life safety, and automation. Electronic security systems have focused on the areas of access control, intrusion detection, and closed-circuit television, as well as integration of these functions with other complex systems that the company supports. The firm has expertise in life safety systems, such as fire detection and alarm, as well as building automation and energy management.

M.C. Dean, Inc. provides construction or renovation of the physical plant—i.e., cabling, pathways, and equipment areas—necessary to implement nearly all advanced system technologies used in today's large buildings and campuses. M.C. Dean, Inc. possesses extensive experience and technical knowledge of the latest design, installation, and construction techniques necessary to ensure an effective physical plant.

QUALITY ASSURANCE

M.C. Dean, Inc. would not be where it is today without the quality assurance it provides all

clients. Total quality is not a cliché at the firm; it is built into every phase of all projects. As evidence, the company recently received the highest award given to private industry by the U.S. Navy for projects completed at a regional facility.

M.C. Dean, Inc.'s technicians are primarily licensed journeymen electricians who have completed four years or more in a federally approved electrical apprenticeship program. Furthermore, most receive specialized classroom and factory training on many of the systems the company services.

M.C. Dean, Inc. regularly holds in-house training on subjects such as fiber optics, high-voltage cabling, and electrical testing. This training affords employees a greater variety of work skills and helps to ensure opportunities for excellence in the technical field of their choice.

"What's made us successful can be attributed to one thing more than any other," says William Dean. "Our average senior manager has 18 years with this firm. Our average field superintendent has 14 years with this firm. So, what you have is an organization that's built around people that have grown up here."

M.C. DEAN, INC.'S SAFETY MANAGER CONDUCTS A JOB-SITE SAFETY MEETING AT THE ONGOING NEW MIDFIELD CONCOURSE-SYSTEMS INTEGRATION PROJECT AT WASHINGTON DULLES INTERNATIONAL AIRPORT.

M.C. DEAN, INC.'S FIELD STAFF ARE PRIMARILY LICENSED JOURNEYMEN AND COMMUNICATIONS TECHNICIANS SKILLED IN STATE-OF-THE-ART TECHNOLOGY. LONGEVITY SPEAKS VOLUMES: MOST SUPERVISORS AND MANAGERS HAVE BEEN WITH THE FIRM FOR MORE THAN A DOZEN YEARS.

THE FUTURE

In the past half century, M.C. Dean, Inc. has evolved into a regional powerhouse in the communications, electronics, and electrical industries, proving its flexibility and adaptability to changing times, as well as to increasingly complex technological and construction demands.

The company continues to look for ways to better serve its customers. Says William Dean, "I would expect in the near future for our customers to be able to contact us via a Web site to initiate a service call. Eventually, the systems that we provide to clients will automatically contact us to initiate service calls, hopefully before the customer even knows they have a problem. These are the types of things we're looking at. This is where we want to be."

Dickstein Shapiro Morin & Oshinsky LLP is a Washington-based law firm dedicated to innovative approaches to problem solving. Clients benefit from the firm's ability to see complex issues clearly and implement successful strategies. Attorneys at Dickstein Shapiro Morin & Oshinsky value the kind of creative thinking that converts obstacles into opportunities. To effectively communicate with clients, Dickstein Shapiro Morin & Oshinsky is equipped with the latest communication technology and computer software, and interacts with clients around the world by electronic means. Dickstein Shapiro Morin & Oshinsky also prides itself on its attorneys and support staff, who are client oriented, decisive, and innovative thinkers.

The firm began in 1953 in New York City, when Sidney Dickstein and David Shapiro joined forces to focus on civil liberties law, especially in defense of McCarthy-era targets of loyalty and security investigations. In 1956, the firm relocated to Washington, and in 1972, Charles Morin—a prominent corporate lawyer from Boston—and his colleagues joined the firm, adding corporate, securities, and banking expertise. The firm continued to expand into a full-service firm, providing comprehensive legal representation to clients. In 1996, premier insurance litigation attorney Jerold Oshinsky and his team joined the firm.

FOUNDING PARTNER SIDNEY DICKSTEIN (LEFT) AND MANAGING PARTNER ANGELO V. ARCADIPANE STAND AT THE ENTRANCE TO THE FIRM'S 2101 L STREET OFFICE.

DICKSTEIN SHAPIRO MORIN & OSHINSKY OCCUPIES APPROXIMATELY 80 PERCENT OF THE 10-FLOOR BUILDING AT 2101 L STREET NW. FOR CLIENT CONVENIENCE, THE FIRM UTILIZES A CENTRALIZED RECEPTION AREA ON THE EIGHTH FLOOR.

Dickstein Shapiro Morin & Oshinsky's commitment to providing comprehensive, quality service to clients—combined with an efficient management philosophy—enables the firm to boast four decades of continuous growth. Now the seventh-largest law firm in Washington, Dickstein Shapiro Morin & Oshinsky currently employs 500 people including 215 attorneys. The firm also services clients through its offices in New York City and St. Petersburg, Russia.

DIVERSITY OF SERVICES

Dickstein Shapiro Morin & Oshinsky recognizes that changing times require creative solutions. Traditional approaches to legal challenges are often inadequate to the task. Dickstein Shapiro Morin & Oshinsky's attorneys have not only the necessary skills and experience, but also the dedication to use those skills and experience to maximize the probability of success. The firm's litigation strategies are designed not just to win in court, but to

better position clients after the dispute is resolved. In transactions, the firm helps clients take advantage of changing market conditions, and in government advocacy, the firm employs innovative strategies to succeed where others have encountered frustration.

Dickstein Shapiro Morin & Oshinsky hosts one of the most diverse practices in Washington. The firm is prepared to efficiently and effectively service clients by utilizing the resources of its 17 practice areas, comprised of bankruptcy and creditor's rights, business crimes/regulatory enforcement, civil litigation, communications, corporate, government affairs, energy, environment and natural resources, financial institutions and real estate, government contracts, intellectual property, international trade and transactions, insurance, labor/general litigation, public sector litigation, securities litigation, and tax.

Dickstein Shapiro Morin & Oshinsky's premier litigation attorneys represent corporations

large and small, government officials, and individuals in civil litigation, criminal, and administrative proceedings and investigations. Dickstein Shapiro Morin & Oshinsky has represented government officials and White House staff during investigations by special prosecutors and congressional committees including Watergate, Koreagate, Iran-Contra, Ill Winds, and Drexel Burnham Lambert prosecutions. Firm engagements have also included key role representation in litigation arising out of the *Exxon Valdez* oil spill; representation as counsel to corporations in connection with initial public offerings; and representation of 31 states in *Delaware v. New York*, a suit with original jurisdiction in the Supreme Court involving $1 billion in unclaimed dividends and other distributions on securities.

Dickstein Shapiro Morin & Oshinsky takes advantage of its location in the nation's capital to service a wide variety of clients in navigating the federal regulatory process. From securing energy resources for international clients to Superfund cleanups and hazardous waste problems, Dickstein Shapiro Morin & Oshinsky's attorneys implement innovative solutions to energy and environmental problems.

The firm represents national investment banking firms, serves as an adviser to one of the nation's largest complexes of mutual funds, and represents several leveraged buyout funds in acquisitions and sales of industrial corporations and corporate divisions. Dickstein Shapiro Morin & Oshinsky also acts as general counsel for more than a dozen corporations located throughout the United States. Dickstein Shapiro Morin & Oshinsky's insurance litigation attorneys represent large industrial policyholders, small companies, utilities, municipalities, state governments, and charities in actions against their insurance companies for insurance coverage.

Recognizing the global economy that exists today, Dickstein Shapiro Morin & Oshinsky's international trade attorneys specialize in, among other things, export and import interests dealing with cross-border transactions, anti-dumping regulations, and administrative reviews before the U.S. Department of Commerce and the International Trade Commission. The firm regularly advises clients on customs and administration laws, providing comprehensive legal advice on international issues.

TECHNOLOGY

The technological revolution creates interesting challenges for legal firms facing the 21st century. Dickstein Shapiro Morin & Oshinsky's attorneys possess the expertise critical in navigating the demands of the high-tech, mass media age. The firm provides clients with strategic business and legal advice in the intellectual property, government contracts, and communications fields. Representation includes intellectual property rights protections, channel sales, licensing issues, bid preparations, negotiations and representation before the Federal Communications Commission, and development of strategies for new ventures in emerging industries.

Dickstein Shapiro Morin & Oshinsky's attorneys understand that clients face fierce competition, rapidly changing technology, and complex government regulation. By providing such a diverse range of services, a wide variety of legal expertise, and a problem-solving philosophy that goes beyond the boundaries of traditional rigid thinking, Dickstein Shapiro Morin & Oshinsky stands ready to provide exceptional legal representation to its clients well into the next century.

CLOCKWISE FROM TOP LEFT:
THE FIRM'S LIBRARY SERVES AS
A RESOURCE CENTER FOR BOTH
ATTORNEYS AND CLIENTS.

DICKSTEIN SHAPIRO MORIN &
OSHINSKY'S OFFICES ARE EQUIPPED
WITH MULTIMEDIA CONFERENCE
ROOMS TO CREATE A COMFORTABLE
WORKING ATMOSPHERE FOR CLIENT
MEETINGS.

DICKSTEIN SHAPIRO MORIN &
OSHINSKY'S RECEPTION AREA IS
DECORATED WITH VIBRANT COLORS,
INCLUDING SUCH WORKS OF ART AS
THE *Ruby Red Macchia*, DESIGNED
BY DALE CHIHULY.

HARACTERISTIC OF THE CITY IN WHICH IT WAS FOUNDED nearly 40 years ago—where actions taken today have repercussions that are felt around the world tomorrow—Verner Liipfert Bernhard McPherson and Hand, Chartered is a firm with both Washington expertise and global reach. ◆ Verner Liipfert complements its capabilities as a results-oriented, full-service law firm by drawing upon members of the firm who

THE FOUNDING MEMBERS—BERL BERNHARD, HARRY MCPHERSON, AND LLOYD HAND—SERVED IN THE WHITE HOUSE AND MAINTAIN ACTIVE NATIONAL AND INTERNATIONAL, WASHINGTON-BASED PRACTICES (TOP RIGHT).

VERNER LIIPFERT'S WASHINGTON OFFICE IS LOCATED IN THE MCPHERSON BUILDING (LEFT AND BOTTOM RIGHT).

have served at the highest levels of government. The firm's former public officials include Treasury Secretary and Senator Lloyd Bentsen, Republican Presidential Nominee and Senate Majority Leader Bob Dole, Senate Majority Leader George Mitchell, Ambassador to Canada and Michigan Governor James Blanchard, Texas Governor Ann Richards, and Hawaii Governor John Waihee. Additionally, others in the firm have served as White House counsel, assistant secretary of state, U.S. chief of protocol, assistant U.S. trade representative, chairman of the Department of Transportation's Commercial Space Transportation Advisory Committee, and member of the Defense Base Closure Commission. Additionally, the three practicing shareholders for whom the firm is named—Berl Bernhard, Harry McPherson, and Lloyd Hand—each served in the White House and maintain active national and international, Washington-based practices.

Legal issues are no longer contested solely in conventional legal arenas, but also before federal agencies and departments, on Capitol Hill, and in the media. In recognition of this new reality, Verner Liipfert provides counsel on the legal, political, regulatory, business, and media components of every issue to achieve positive results for its clients.

The firm represents more than 90 of the Fortune 500 companies; numerous other local, national, and international corporations; trade associations; nonprofit organizations; and a number of

ROSS STANSFIELD

state, local, and foreign governments. Its more than 170 attorneys and consultants specialize in over 25 substantive practice areas including antitrust and trade regulation; communications; corporate, securities, and finance; employment and labor; energy (electric, natural gas, and petroleum); environment; estate planning and probate; financial restructuring and bankruptcy; government procurement and dispute resolution; health care; insurance; international; federal and legislative affairs; civil and criminal litigation; privatization; real estate; state and local government; solid waste, water, and wastewater facility development; tax; and transportation (aviation, maritime, and surface).

In addition to Washington, the firm's offices in McLean, Virginia; Houston and Austin, Texas; and Honolulu enable Verner Liipfert to reach beyond the beltway to serve its clients' needs, nationally and throughout the world.

Described in the *Washington Post* as one "of the city's most influential law firms," Verner Liipfert's attorneys have assisted clients with matters ranging from routine transactions and minor

legislative fixes to major mergers and acquisitions and large-scale, multifaceted campaigns to shape public policy. The firm, for example, has formed and led coalitions, including an effort to amend tax laws affecting the health care, insurance, finance, and education industries that helped build bipartisan consensus in favor of Verner Liipfert's clients' positions.

The firm's mergers and acquisition expertise was highlighted in *MediaWeek* magazine on February 5, 1996. Its cover story, "Media's Mr. Fix-It," was subtitled, "With clients such as Disney, NBC, Viacom, and Westinghouse, attorney Berl Bernhard is the man to know in D.C. . . . Verner Liipfert is positioned better than anyone

in New York or L.A. to make things happen."

Verner Liipfert's knowledge of Washington's institutions, the government officials who lead them, and the broad policy considerations that can lead to the successful resolution of matters on its clients' behalf is supplemented by the firm's dedication to "thinking outside the box."

The ability to find a solution where none seems to exist—to make use of its considerable resources creatively—is what sets Verner Liipfert apart from other firms in the nation's capital. Its full-service capabilities in dozens of practice areas, coupled with the strategic value of offices across the country, are what places Verner Liipfert in a class of its own.

CLOCKWISE FROM TOP LEFT: SENATE MAJORITY LEADER GEORGE MITCHELL AND TREASURY SECRETARY AND SENATOR LLOYD BENTSEN ARE AMONG THE FIRM'S MEMBERS WHO HAVE SERVED AS PUBLIC OFFICIALS.

SENATOR BOB DOLE WITH MEMBERS OF VERNER LIIPFERT'S EXECUTIVE COMMITTEE: LENARD PARKINS, JAMES HIBEY, AMY BONDURANT, AND CLINTON VINCE. JOSEPH MANSON NOT AVAILABLE FOR PHOTOGRAPH.

THE FIRM'S FORMER PUBLIC OFFICIALS INCLUDE AMBASSADOR TO CANADA AND MICHIGAN GOVERNOR JAMES BLANCHARD, TEXAS GOVERNOR ANN RICHARDS, AND HAWAII GOVERNOR JOHN WAIHEE.

MARK BORCHELT

UCH LIKE THE FOOD SERVED IN ITS RESTAURANTS EACH summer, Clyde's Restaurant Group is homegrown. Starting with one restaurant in 1963, the group now owns nine restaurants that are part of one of the area's top-grossing restaurant companies. ♦ Thinking Washington lacked a good saloon, Harvard graduate, World War II pilot, and international businessman Stuart Davidson opened Clyde's in 1963. Six months later, John Laytham, who was a foreign service major at Georgetown University, started to work at Clyde's as a busboy. This unlikely pair of restaurateurs ultimately launched one of the most enduring and successful restaurant companies in the United States.

Washington didn't have anything like Clyde's in the early 1960s. Restrictive liquor laws had been repealed and the town was full of interesting people drawn to the nation's capital during the Kennedy administration, yet there was no gathering spot. Davidson filled the void by offering a comfortable and unpretentious place with good drinks and simple, high-quality food. Clyde's of Georgetown was an immediate success.

The Old Ebbitt Grill, Washington's oldest saloon, dating back to 1856, became the second venture for the two owners. In 1970, they attended an Internal Revenue Service auction at the Ebbitt, as the result of a federal tax lien, hoping to acquire its collection of antique beer steins for Clyde's. Several hours later, they successfully bid on the entire operation. Today, the Old Ebbitt Grill ranks among the top-grossing independently owned restaurants in the nation.

In 1975, Clyde's opened a restaurant in Columbia, Maryland, and in 1980, a Clyde's opened in Tysons Corner. In 1985, Clyde's bought three existing restaurants near Georgetown University, including 1789 Restaurant, one of the city's finest. In the 1990s, Clyde's has opened restaurants in Reston, Virginia, and Chevy Chase, Maryland. In addition, the Ebbitt Express, adjacent to the Old Ebbitt Grill, now offers freshly prepared carryout food.

Clyde's has resisted offers to expand beyond the capital region. Clyde's Restaurant Group already employs more than 1,300 Washington-area residents, and as the expansion continues, that number is expected to grow.

HOMEGROWN FRESH

For nearly a decade, Clyde's Restaurant Group has had its own homegrown produce program. Fresh fruits and vegetables, grown especially for Clyde's by local farmers, are delivered daily to the restaurants from spring until fall.

Clyde's started buying food from local farmers in the late 1980s. Although it's more expensive than importing foods from other parts of the country, Laytham, who is now executive vice president, says the freshness pays off by creating return customers. He says, "We figured, why use a pink tomato from Florida when there are so many wonderful things growing around us?"

Fresh-picked produce is used in everything from salsa to fruit cobblers and pies. Each winter, Clyde's chefs meet with local farmers to plan the next year's crops, sometimes putting in special orders for foods featured in the restaurants' menus.

It's that attention to detail that has helped Clyde's grow into a successful restaurant enterprise. And it's Clyde's Restaurant Group's commitment to this region that allows Washington-area residents and visitors to feast on the homegrown foods expertly prepared by employees of this homegrown business.

CLYDE'S ACQUIRED THE OLD EBBITT GRILL, WASHINGTON'S OLDEST SALOON, DATING BACK TO 1856, IN 1970. TODAY THE OLD EBBITT GRILL RANKS AMONG THE TOP-GROSSING INDEPENDENTLY OWNED RESTAURANTS IN THE NATION (LEFT).

LIKE ALL RESTAURANTS IN THE CLYDE'S FAMILY, CLYDE'S OF CHEVY CHASE OFFERS A COMFORTABLE AND UNPRETENTIOUS PLACE WITH GOOD DRINKS AND SIMPLE, HIGH-QUALITY FOOD (RIGHT).

WASHINGTON'S DOWNTOWN DISTRICT IS IN A RENAISSANCE period that has revitalized the area's business and entertainment industry, and marked a new beginning for an old hotel. The Hotel Anthony, founded in 1965, was renamed the Lincoln Suites Downtown after the completion of a $1.5 million renovation. December of 1995 marked the real beginning of change for the hotel when Hospitality Partners became the new owners and management of the hotel.

THE LINCOLN SUITES' MISSION

Hospitality Partners stresses to its employees that their mission is "to create a welcoming environment, create an informative environment, create an entertaining environment, and create a caring and hassle-free environment without forgetting to collect the cash."

ACCOMPLISHING THE MISSION

Each of the 99 classically remodeled studio suites is equipped with either a wet bar or a full kitchen. The hotel staff strives to provide a clean, comfortable, and friendly environment for all guests. The knowledgeable staff provides information on Washington-area restaurants and night life. They also aid tourists in making informed decisions on what to see and do so they don't get lost in the vast Washington attractions. The hotel makes guests feel welcomed at check-in with a sit-down front desk. They are happy to spend time with the guests, answering any questions about the hotel and the city. Guests lucky enough to be checking in around 5 p.m. are met at the door by the sweet smell of freshly baked cookies. The staff serves the cookies (and milk, of course) each evening in the lobby.

A CENTRAL LOCATION

Located in the heart of the downtown business, historic, and entertainment district, the

R.O. FRASIER

Lincoln Suites is just blocks from many of the city's monuments and tourist attractions. The White House is just five blocks and the Mall is only seven blocks away. The fantastic location provides guests with easy access to Washington's Metro, which makes traveling in the city a breeze. The hotel is just one and a half blocks away from the Farragut North (Red line) and Farragut West (Orange and Blue lines) Metro stations.

The hotel's neighborhood is full of quaint pubs and restaurants, offering a wide variety of cuisine. The Beatrice Restaurant provides room service for the hotel's guests,

featuring authentic Italian cuisine. Guests are provided with a downtown restaurant guide that outlines the cuisine and operating hours of area restaurants, or guests can ask the expert hotel staff for dining advice. Additionally, the hotel's guest services directory, complete with addresses and phone numbers, is a hassle-free way for guests to map out area restaurants, shops, and services.

Lincoln Suites staff and management are dedicated to fulfilling their mission of providing guests with a welcoming, informative, entertaining, caring, and hassle-free environment.

LOCATED IN THE HEART OF THE DOWNTOWN BUSINESS, HISTORIC, AND ENTERTAINMENT DISTRICT, THE LINCOLN SUITES IS JUST BLOCKS FROM MANY OF THE CITY'S MONUMENTS AND TOURIST ATTRACTIONS. ALL SUITES HAVE A TELEPHONE WITH DATA PORTS AND VOICE MAIL, COFFEE/TEA MAKER, MICROWAVE, REFRIGERATOR, REMOTE CONTROL TELEVISION WITH FREE HBO, IN-ROOM MOVIES, AND NINTENDO.

THE STORY OF HOW EROL'S BECAME ONE OF THE TOP INTERNET providers in the Washington area is an evolutionary tale. From its modest beginnings as a television and radio repair shop, the company grew, first, to become the largest video rental and sales enterprise in the United States, and then to its current position as a leading Internet provider. This is also the story of how a young emigrant from

Turkey achieved the American dream.

Erol Onaran left Turkey in 1960 with $32 in his pocket, and by the time the television repairman arrived in the United States, he had $16 left. Today his son, Orhan, is president of Erol's Internet, which—after only one and a half years in business—has achieved more than 200,000 subscribers. During its first year, the company became the eighth-largest on-line service provider in the country.

THE HISTORY

In 1963, Erol's started as a television and radio repair shop. Erol Onaran expanded the business to include television sales in 1967, and in 1976 Erol's began

to sell the machine that would change the world of entertainment forever—the videocassette recorder (VCR).

The 1980s were very good for Erol's. The decade began with the birth of Erol's Video Club, which became the largest video club in the country. As the company grew, Onaran noted, "I don't do this to make money. I do this to make fun." Nonetheless, the business made money. The chain grew to 220 stores before it was sold to Blockbuster for $30 million in 1991.

Tired of being away from the customers, Onaran and his son bought back the TV/VCR Service Department from Blockbuster in 1992. Later in the year, Erol's returned to selling televisions and

VCRs, and the familiar Washington institution of Erol's customer service was back.

Erol's did not rest on its laurels. Always a company on the cutting edge, Erol's began building and selling computers in April 1994. With constant attention to meeting each customer's needs, Erol's produced custom-built computers for its clientele and, once again, set the standard by which customer service should be judged.

In August 1995, the company entered what has since become its fastest-growing endeavor: the Internet. The company's goal was to bring Erol's service into homes across the region and become the Internet provider of choice by guaranteeing unbeatable low

ORHAN ONARAN (RIGHT), SON OF EROL ONARAN, IS FOUNDER OF EROL'S INTERNET. DENNIS SPINA SERVES AS CEO.

prices, high volume, and unparalleled customer service.

A Golden Philosophy

At Erol's, the business philosophy is simple: The customer comes first, employees come second, suppliers come third, and the owner comes last. It's a philosophy that Onaran had when he started his business, and it has served him well for more than three decades. The philosophy of the founder of Erol's is a perfect formula for customer satisfaction, and Erol's Internet proves it every day. The Erol's guarantee promises that if for any reason a customer is not satisfied, he or she will receive a full refund within 30 days and a prorated refund every day thereafter.

Correcting technical and operational problems has become the company's number one priority. A constant quest for customer satisfaction has also prompted Erol's to recruit the most talented Internet staff available. The bottom line at Erol's is that there's no excuse for customer dissatisfaction.

Erol's Internet Services

The demand for Erol's service is staggering. The company establishes nearly 20,000 new accounts per month currently in the mid-Atlantic and in the recently targeted Northeast region. After having trouble keeping up with

demand for its services during its first couple of months, the company now stands poised for expansion. "People say, 'Why are you growing so fast?' I don't have a choice," says Orhan Onaran.

Such growth has come with a price. Occasionally, demand has surpassed the company's ability to serve. Orhan Onaran admits that he is never content in the area of customer service. "I'm not satisfied yet," he says. "We're good. But we've got to become the best out there."

Erol's low-priced connection fees and customer-oriented technical support team generate a lot of customer loyalty. To all its customers, Erol's remains "The Best Value on the Net."

Erol's Internet has successfully marketed its services with newspaper and magazine ads and a flood of television and radio spots. The company has also attracted

numerous subscribers through word-of-mouth recommendations. Vending carts at malls throughout the firm's coverage umbrella also allow potential customers to take a free ride in surfing the Internet. All of Erol's products and services may also be purchased at these sites.

Erol's reputation rests on total dedication to superior customer service. Since the company was founded in 1963, excellent customer service has been Erol's most constant product. While engineering a corporate vision and building its infrastructure, Erol's designed customer satisfaction into every element of the business. And, as always, this customer satisfaction is guaranteed.

What does the future hold for Erol's? Orhan Onaran says the future is bright: "We are just getting started. The potential is awesome."

CLOCKWISE FROM TOP LEFT: A CONSTANT QUEST FOR CUSTOMER SATISFACTION HAS PROMPTED EROL'S TO RECRUIT THE MOST TALENTED INTERNET STAFF AVAILABLE. DENNIS SPINA (CENTER), REMAINS AVAILABLE FOR STAFF CONSULTATION.

FROM ITS MODEST BEGINNINGS IN 1963 AS A TELEVISION AND RADIO REPAIR SHOP, EROL'S GREW, FIRST, TO BECOME THE LARGEST VIDEO RENTAL AND SALES ENTERPRISE IN THE UNITED STATES, AND THEN TO ITS CURRENT POSITION AS A LEADING INTERNET PROVIDER.

AFTER ITS FIRST YEAR AND A HALF IN BUSINESS, EROL'S INTERNET ACHIEVED MORE THAN 200,000 SUBSCRIBERS, AND A CAKE WAS MADE TO HONOR THE OCCASION.

THE COMPUCARE COMPANY

OR ALMOST THREE DECADES, HUNDREDS OF HOSPITALS HAVE benefited from Compucare's expertise in information systems consulting, information systems strategic planning, facilities management, and turnkey hospital information systems. And as the industry has grown and evolved, so has Compucare. Headquartered in Reston, Virginia, Compucare Company is a recognized innovator in health care information systems.

Compucare employs more than 200 health care and information systems professionals who design and support information management applications for health care providers and their affiliates in the United States and Canada.

A NEW GENERATION OF PRODUCTS

Released in 1992, the Affinity™ product is a technologically advanced health care information system (HCIS) designed and constructed by industry experts. Representative of an evolution of ideas and functionality, Affinity was designed, developed, and released during the dynamic era of managed care, consolidation and merger of hospitals, and stringent continuum of care requirements. Unlike older-generation HCIS systems designed in the 1970s and 1980s, Affinity is designed to meet the demands of health care organizations today, as well as those of the next century. As the nature and demand for information changes within the health care industry, Affinity assures the ability to meet these new challenges facing health care organizations.

Comprised of more than 25 fully integrated applications, Affinity provides a comprehensive range of market-leader products. The spectrum of applications, from Patient Financial Management and Patient Information Management to Patient Care Management, is centric-designed around Affinity's patient-centered database. Providing seamless access to information throughout the health care network, Affinity emphasizes the integration of key clinical, financial, and administrative data through adherence to structural query language (SQL) industry standards. Affinity's open database connectivity (ODBC) compliant, patient-centered database is the keystone of a patient's electronic medical record.

ACCESS TO INFORMATION FOR BETTER DECISIONS, BETTER CARE

Affinity supplies innovative solutions that are hardware independent. Available on Windows NT or UNIX platforms, both hardware and software provide open access to information and are capable of expansion as a health care organization grows and business needs change. As the first HCIS vendor to incorporate intranet, Web-browser technology within business applications, Affinity is positioned as the information hub in an enterprise-wide environment.

DESIGNED BY USERS FOR USERS

All of Affinity's application screens are displayed visually using a graphical user interface (GUI). Intuitive to the end user, point-and-click navigation ensures ease of entry and output. Through the use of client design and test groups known as developmental partners, Affinity's applications are, in essence, designed by the end user for the end user. Pragmatic, functional applications are the end result. Affinity customers receive robust applications that meet their business needs, whether those needs are in the financial area or in delivering quality patient care.

Leadership in software to support health care delivery is Compucare's goal for tomorrow. By excelling in development and installation of software to meet the needs of hospitals and emerging delivery networks, the company is well positioned to continue its growth and success.

FOR NEARLY THREE DECADES, EU SERVICES HAS BEEN RECOGNIZED by its customers, industry peers, and community as one of the finest full-service printing and mailing companies in the country. Established in Rockville, Maryland, in 1968, the company now employs more than 425 people. Each division of EU Services has extensive products and services rarely matched in the industry and operates 24 hours a day to meet the tight schedules of its customers.

"Coordinating products and services to produce efficient, timely, and cost-saving direct mail packages requires extensive products and services, a sophisticated communication network, and staff expertise," explains President and Board Chairman J. Bruce Mackey. "Constant communication between production management and our project coordinators helps to keep projects on track, regardless of the inevitable changes that occur during production," says Mackey. "The invisible web of communication synergy, together with our extensive technical knowledge of how products and services interrelate, enables us to produce the most complicated projects on time, within budget, and with the desired quality expected of us."

BUSINESS PHILOSOPHY

EU Services' values were first articulated by the company founder, John C. Mackey, when he said, "Do everything in your power to give the highest level of service to every one of our customers. And at all times be fair, be courteous, be friendly, and be responsible." The company continues to be true to its founder's vision and values.

"Customers can feel secure that no matter how difficult or demanding a project, we will do everything in our power to produce it the way they want it, when they want it, within their budget, and in an atmosphere of professionalism and uncommon friendliness," Mackey pledges.

COMMUNITY COMMITMENT

EU Services remains committed to the community in which it was founded. Employees are encouraged to voluntarily participate in company-sponsored civic campaigns like the EU Caring Campaign. The primary mission of the Caring Campaign has always been to help families in need within the local community. At any given time, the program may provide financial and emotional support during the course of the year to up to 20 families.

Local students benefit from the Caring Campaign's Scholarship Fund. In addition, dozens of families are helped each year with small donations of food coupons or checks to landlords or utility companies to prevent evictions and service cutoffs.

The Caring Campaign also supports nonprofit organizations within the community, including the Make-A-Wish Foundation of Rockville, Hispanics United for Rockville, the Helping Hands Shelter for Abused Women, and Hospice Caring.

EU Services strives to employ people with good character, who possess a strong work ethic and who will commit themselves to the business, its customers, and the community.

CLOCKWISE FROM TOP: PRESIDENT AND CHAIRMAN J. BRUCE MACKEY (LEFT) AND EXECUTIVE VICE PRESIDENT JOHN LOUDON OVERSEE EU SERVICES, ONE OF THE FINEST FULL-SERVICE PRINTING AND MAILING COMPANIES IN THE COUNTRY. THEY STAND BEFORE A PORTRAIT OF JOHN C. MACKEY, EU SERVICES' FOUNDER.

AN ENTIRE DEPARTMENT OF DESKTOP WORK STATIONS, WORKING THREE SHIFTS A DAY, FIVE TO SEVEN DAYS A WEEK, PROVIDES THE CAPACITY TO ACCOMMODATE EVERY CUSTOMER NEED.

MULTI-UNIT WEB PRESSES PRINT UP TO 2.5 MILLION IMPRESSIONS A DAY.

O NE OF THE LEADING INFORMATION TECHNOLOGY COMPANIES IN the federal government marketplace, Federal Data Corporation was the first systems integrator and continues to be at the forefront of the industry. Classified as a small business, the privately held company has nonetheless had a big impact, with a long history of providing innovative systems and solutions for

ROBERT HANLEY, FOUNDER AND CHAIRMAN EMERITUS OF FEDERAL DATA CORPORATION, STANDS WITH HIS ENTREPRENEUR OF THE YEAR AWARD. HANLEY IS PROUD OF THE PROFOUND IMPACT THE COMPANY HAS HAD ON THE FEDERAL GOVERN-MENT INFORMATION TECHNOLOGY MARKETPLACE (LEFT).

DAN YOUNG, FEDERAL DATA PRESI-DENT AND CEO, REGARDS THE FUTURE WITH OPTIMISM. THE COMPANY THRIVES ON NEW IDEAS, NEW TECHNOLOGIES, AND NEW APPLICATIONS—AND RELIES ON TRADITIONAL STRENGTHS (RIGHT).

customers in both the public and private sectors. The company's commitment to its customers is paramount. Whether designing computer or network solutions or providing professional services, technical support, or end user applications training, Federal Data seeks to understand its customers' specific needs and respond to them.

The founder and chairman emeritus of Federal Data Corporation, Robert Hanley, started the company with this idea in mind in 1969 and served as its president until 1985, when he became its chairman and chief executive officer. He held that position until January 1996, shortly after Federal Data was acquired by the Carlyle Group, a Washington-based private merchant bank, which has been an active investor in the aerospace/defense and information technol-

ogy areas for many years. Hanley continues to serve as a member of the board of directors and as a consultant to the company.

Dan Young joined the company in 1976 as its executive vice president and has served as a director since 1977. Assuming the role of president when Hanley stepped aside in 1985, he also filled Hanley's shoes as CEO in January 1996.

Federal Data Corporation strives to be the best, not necessarily biggest, player in its field. While growth has been an important part of the company's nearly 30-year history, that growth has not come at the expense of quality, according to Young. He regards the company's reputation as one of its greatest assets. "Federal Data will continue to ensure quality performance in the present that reaches or surpasses standards set in the past," Young explains. "We won't sacrifice quality for quantity."

A FEDERAL ALLIANCE

B ecause the federal government is such a sophisticated user of high technology, providing cost-effective, leading-edge systems solutions has been an exciting challenge for Federal Data and is the basis on which the company was founded. Hanley was a true pioneer in this arena. His experience working for Control Data Corporation and other firms in the Washington area during the late 1960s convinced him that the rapid development of technologically superior information processing equipment was outstripping the manufacturing community's ability to sell it to the federal government. In a market dominated by large manufacturers offering conventional leasing programs limiting their subscribers to their own product lines, Hanley believed that a single prime contractor offering solutions responsive to a cus-

JOHN WHITMAN

tomer's technical and financial needs would be an attractive alternative.

The availability of high-quality, commercial, off-the-shelf, plug-compatible equipment made it possible for a prime contractor to package hardware, software, peripherals, and support services from various sources into custom turnkey systems, a process now commonly known as systems integration. Hanley's vision rested on a single strategy: combine technical and financial approaches to win government business. His plan worked. His bold idea transformed the landscape of federal procurement and spawned an entire new industry.

It was Hanley's personal business philosophy, however, that set the tone for a spirit that is evident throughout the company even today. Hanley had two goals for Federal Data: make money and have fun—one being meaningless without the other.

THE ENTREPRENEURIAL SPIRIT

Federal Data is described as a company with "a lot of personality." It is undoubtedly a reflection of the management style of a closely knit group of executives who have set the tone and pace of day-to-day life at the company and earned the respect and support of the employees. And, because Federal Data has resisted growth simply for growth's sake, it has been able to stay entrepreneurial, flexible, and strategically focused.

This attitude is encouraged throughout the company, which thrives on new ideas, new technologies, and new applications. Federal Data believes that giving its employees the impetus to adapt quickly to change is crucial to maintaining a competitive edge. In turn, the employees respond to the excitement and rise to the challenge to stay ahead of the pack.

Those Federal Data employees who consistently produce high-

ERIC TAYLOR, SCULPTURE BY DR. ROBERT TAYLOR

quality work over the years receive the company's highest recognition—the award of an Eagle. It is an acknowledgment of dedication, vision, and achievement. The eagle is an important symbol at Federal Data. Not only is it clearly associated with the federal government, but as a living creature, the eagle possesses many qualities the company admires and emulates. For example, eagles have the sharpest vision in the animal world, with eyesight that is eight times better than a human's. They have the ability to soar more than a thousand feet and, at the same time, see a mouse in the grass from a mile away. An eagle can fly a distance of more than 200 miles a day.

It's easy to make comparisons with these birds of prey and the spirit fostered at Federal Data. Eagles must be alert, agile, decisive, strong, skillful, and persistent to survive. These qualities are prized in the company's employees and reflect the attributes that have made them—and Federal Data—successful.

As Federal Data continues to flourish under Young's leadership, the dawn of the 21st century offers new challenges and opportunities. The company will meet them with it's traditional strengths: integrity, intelligence, creativity, adaptability, and perseverance. Some things just don't change.

THE EAGLE IS AN IMPORTANT SYMBOL AT FEDERAL DATA. THIS LIFE-SIZE BRONZE EAGLE BY SCULPTOR DR. ROBERT TAYLOR STANDS IN THE COMPANY'S HEADQUARTERS IN BETHESDA. EMPLOYEES WHO EARN FEDERAL DATA'S HIGHEST RECOGNITION RECEIVE A BRONZE REPLICA.

1970	AMERICAN MANAGEMENT SYSTEMS, INC.
1970	SYSTEM PLANNING CORPORATION
1971	SOFTWARE AG
1972	THE WATERGATE HOTEL
1972	WHUR-FM
1973	JERRY'S FORD, INC.
1974	ANTIQUE & CONTEMPORARY LEASING AND SALES, INC.
1976	ONE WASHINGTON CIRCLE HOTEL
1978	ELECTRONIC DATA SYSTEMS CORPORATION
1979	FEDDEMAN & COMPANY, P.C.
1980	THE FRED EZRA CO.
1980	KAISER PERMANENTE
1982	BEST SOFTWARE, INC.
1982	NetCom SOLUTIONS INTERNATIONAL, INC.
1982	THE WASHINGTON TIMES
1983	HORIZON DATA CORPORATION
1983	ORACLE CORPORATION
1984	SHERIKON, INC.
1984	TROY SYSTEMS INC.
1986	MELLON, NATIONAL CAPITAL AREA
1987	SYLVEST MANAGEMENT SYSTEMS CORPORATION
1987	SYTEL, INC.
1988	RELIABLE INTEGRATION SERVICES, INC.
1991	UNITEL CORPORATION
1993	SpaceWorks, INC.
1995	AXENT TECHNOLOGIES, INC.
1995	NORTEL COMMUNICATIONS SYSTEMS, INC.
1995	RELIASTAR EMPLOYER FINANCIAL SERVICES COMPANY
1997	J&H MARSH & McLENNAN, INC.

American Management Systems, Inc.

American Management Systems, Inc. (AMS) is an international business and information technology consulting firm headquartered in the Washington metropolitan area with offices in more than 50 cities throughout North America and Europe. AMS partners with clients to achieve breakthrough performance through the intelligent use of information technology. With 27 years of sustained growth, AMS continues its steady progress toward becoming a billion-dollar business.

Trust-Based Relationships and Focused Industry Expertise

The AMS strategy is built on the twin pillars of long-term, trust-based client relationships and leadership in specialized areas of expertise. The company focuses on both the private and public sectors, with expertise in specific industries, including telecommunications, financial services, state and local governments, federal government agencies, educational institutions, insurance, health care, and electric and gas utilities. AMS clients know that AMS will understand their objectives, act to further their interests, and consistently deliver on commitments. This is the heart of AMS's trust-based relationships.

Within the consulting, systems development, and systems integration markets, AMS provides a full complement of services, including strategic consulting, business process reengineering, and technology consulting, as well as systems integration, development, and implementation. This broad range of capabilities enables AMS to partner with clients throughout the process—from defining strategy to implementing systems—to ensure clients achieve their performance goals. AMS's culture places extreme value on successfully completing complex projects on time and within budget.

Linking People, Process, Organization, and Technology

A big part of AMS's success is based on the company's commitment to advise and assist clients in how to use advanced technologies to achieve dramatic performance improvements in their organizations. The achievement of breakthrough performance requires forward-looking but practical ideas for improving business processes; intelligent use of technology to enable improved processes; and committed, trained people in appropriately aligned organizations.

"We know how to intelligently apply the power of information technology," explains AMS Chairman of the Board Charles O. Rossotti. "We think about entire processes to see how our clients can use information technology to produce genuine results. This approach, combined with our deep understanding of the targeted markets we serve, enables us to understand our clients' business environments and to propose visionary business and technology solutions for the future that meet our clients' business goals with acceptable risk and investment."

A Great Place to Work

Making AMS a great place to work is one of the company's top-priority goals. The flexible work environment at AMS has allowed the firm to recruit and retain the best and brightest employees in the industry. To support its growth, the company continues to hire approximately 1,500 new staff members each year, taking pride in the exceptional talents of those hired.

"Since the roots of our culture and our success are our people," says AMS Chief Executive Officer Paul A. Brands, "it's important that we create a working environment that offers challenging work in an entrepreneurial culture. We know that providing a nonbureaucratic workplace with open communication and a supportive environment is the best way to deliver results to clients."

AMS's commitment to helping its people balance their work and personal lives has garnered accolades from *ComputerWorld* and *Working Mother* magazines, both of which rank AMS among their 100 Best Companies. By attracting the most talented and skilled people in the business, AMS is able to provide its clients with high-quality service.

"We think about entire processes to see how our clients can use information technology to produce genuine results," says AMS Chairman of the Board Charles O. Rossotti. "This approach, combined with our deep understanding of the targeted markets we serve, enables us to understand our clients' business environments and to propose visionary business and technology solutions." (left)

"Since the roots of our culture and our success are our people," says AMS Chief Executive Officer Paul A. Brands, "it's important that we create a working environment that offers challenging work in an entrepreneurial culture. We know that providing a nonbureaucratic workplace with open communication and a supportive environment is the best way to deliver results to clients." (right)

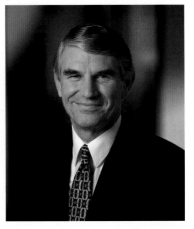

ANTIQUE AND CONTEMPORARY LEASING AND SALES, INC. (ACL) HAS HELD a unique place in Washington's marketplace since 1974. It is the only furniture company in the metropolitan area that specializes in the selling and leasing of high-quality furniture as well as antiques. As a result, its customers have total flexibility in choosing their furniture options. These options generally suit those who move to Washington

knowing they might be moving away, as well as those who eventually decide to stay. In the latter case, customers may lease furniture with an option to buy, allowing themselves the ability to purchase some or all of the furniture at any time. On occasion, those moving overseas like what they have leased so much that they buy a few extra pieces to take with them. ACL offers total flexibility and personal service to satisfy the furnishing needs of its customers.

ACL is located on Capitol Hill in a 100-year-old red brick warehouse. Its two floors are filled with an eclectic mix of furniture, paintings, rugs, and accessories. Those who are searching for an antique armoire, dining table, or oriental rug can be assured that ACL has them. The store's selection of oil paintings and prints includes a series of Hogarth engravings, bird prints, and assorted framed vintage photographs of Washington to make the newcomer feel at home. Khilim, dhurrie, and needlepoint rugs are also included in the inventory. ACL offers antique pine furniture and a variety of Korean furniture, as well.

Furniture from Antique and Contemporary Leasing has been used by such customers as Diana, Princess of Wales; Cher; William Hurt; Jack Nicholson; Peter Jennings; Ted Koppel; and the White House. ACL has furnished everything from $3 million houses for real estate developers to short-term rentals for actors at the Kennedy Center and the Shakespeare Theater. As for movies, set directors often lease furniture from ACL when filming movies in the Washington area.

If a customer needs to rent a chair, special order a sofa, or furnish a guest room, ACL can help. The company slogan is: "If you like what we have, we have a way for you to get it!" Customers love what they find at Antique and Contemporary Leasing, and they always find free parking and a warm welcome inside.

LOCATED ON CAPITOL HILL IN A 100-YEAR-OLD RED BRICK WAREHOUSE, ANTIQUE AND CONTEMPORARY LEASING AND SALES, INC. (ACL) IS THE ONLY FURNITURE COMPANY IN THE METROPOLITAN AREA THAT SPECIALIZES IN THE SELLING AND LEASING OF HIGH-QUALITY FURNITURE AS WELL AS ANTIQUES (TOP).

ACL'S TWO FLOORS ARE FILLED WITH AN ECLECTIC MIX OF FURNITURE, PAINTINGS, RUGS, AND ACCESSORIES. THOSE WHO ARE SEARCHING FOR AN ANTIQUE ARMOIRE, DINING TABLE, OR ORIENTAL RUG CAN BE ASSURED OF FINDING THEM (BOTTOM).

▶ BOB NAROD

FROM DEVELOPING THE HIGH-TECH SECURITY SYSTEMS FOR THE 1996 Summer Olympics in Atlanta to using its expertise in stealth technology, System Planning Corporation is helping the federal government and defense agencies adapt to a rapidly changing world. ◆ System Planning Corporation (SPC) was founded in 1970 by Dr. Ronald L. Easley, a veteran of the Pentagon. His vision was to create an intellectual organization in the Washington area to enhance U.S. security. In the past quarter century, Easley's vision has become reality. "One of the things that makes SPC unique," says Easley, "is that it's a group of people who have come together to serve the country."

SPC was founded as an employee-owned company dedicated to identifying new applications for emerging technologies. The company's charter is to provide superior scientific analysis, systems engineering, and prototype designs for programs addressing critical national requirements.

SPC has sustained steady growth over the past 25 years. Sales for 1996 approached $50 million, and the company employs nearly 300 people. SPC's customer base includes many federal, state, and local government agencies, more than 100 leading aerospace and industrial firms, international business and industrial clients, and allied and friendly foreign governments. The objective in each project for SPC is simple: to provide the customer with a quality of service or product that meets all requirements and expectations within budget and on time.

DOD ALLY

The centers of excellence in SPC's organizational structure reveal the company's close association with the Department of Defense (DOD). Centers for Intelligence, Advanced Technology, and Systems Engineering specialize in supporting emerging technology development programs. Principal customers are the Defense Advanced Research Projects Agency, Ballistic Missile Defense Organization, Defense Special Weapons Agency, and the intelligence community.

The Radar Physics Center and Signature and Electronic Warfare Center are the company's focal point for programs relating to stealth and counterstealth technologies. The Information Technology Center applies information technologies to meet the requirements of operating programs and facilities. The range of services and products are used to enhance the efficiency and effectiveness of vital support functions, such as security, facilities management, and computer center operations.

Although DOD continues to be SPC's largest customer, the company also provides client services to other government agencies, including the intelligence community, the National Aeronautics and Space Administration (NASA), the Federal Emergency Management Agency, and the National Park Service. In the private sector, SPC serves a diverse group of the nation's largest aerospace firms, research laboratories, and Fortune 500 companies.

STEALTH DEVELOPMENT

In the 1970s, SPC pioneered the design and fabrication of precision instrumentation measurement radars to evaluate the radio frequency (RF) signature of low-observable objects. The company's five generations of radars are now installed throughout the country in government and major aerospace company ranges.

"We built the best radar that was possible," says Easley. "It was needed to see literally bug-sized objects, and no one had done that before."

FOUNDER RONALD L. EASLEY SERVES AS CHAIRMAN OF THE BOARD OF SYSTEM PLANNING CORPORATION.

◀ WAYNE HILL

SPC applies signature warfare technology concepts to enhance the effectiveness and survivability of naval ships and aircraft in a variety of warfare areas and threatening environments. Signature control is one of the defense-critical technologies designated by the Secretary of Defense for maintaining the qualitative superiority of U.S. weapon systems.

Another of SPC's successes is TAClink, a datalink mounted on a helicopter that allows surveillance of events up to 60 miles away. In addition to the military application of tactical reconnaissance, TAClink can assist on manhunts and surveillance for the war on drugs.

As risks to national defense change, SPC is accepting the fresh challenges that require innovative solutions. In an atmosphere of downsizing and streamlining, SPC is putting tools into the hands of decision makers to help them decide how to address national security concerns effectively as they reengineer the government.

SECURITY

Providing national security today includes providing Americans with a sense of personal security. As concern in the United States grows over terrorism, private corporations such as SPC are increasingly called upon to help develop the technologies that will secure a peaceful tomorrow.

SPC focuses on applying state-of-the-art computing technology to the management of major facilities and programs. Specializing in the design and installation of electronic security systems, the company was a key security contractor for the 1996 Summer Olympics in Atlanta.

Another program includes design and installation of the advanced entry control system (AECS), which will be the only access control system certified to protect nuclear weapons. SPC provides computer-aided design and drafting and engineering services to NASA's Goddard Space Flight Center, and designed the automated inventory and condition assessment system for the National Park Service. SPC is also a leader in the area of emergency management. Its staff helped develop the National Security Emergency Plan and the family of plans for all emergencies requiring a federal response. SPC conducted after-action reports following the Midwest floods of 1993, hurricanes Hugo and Andrew, and the Northridge earthquake.

THE FUTURE

SPC thrives on its adaptability to change. New products include development of electric vehicles, as well as services and custom solutions to Internet service organizations and users. The company's future includes providing support for developing new uses for the World Wide Web.

SPC's ability to quickly adapt to a changing world will keep the company going strong. "If you're very good, and you're smart, and you're small, there's plenty of things to do," says Easley. "Actually, it's a good time for us."

SOFTWARE AG

ONE OF THE LARGEST INDEPENDENT SOFTWARE FIRMS IN THE world, SOFTWARE AG creates technology-based tools and solutions that help customers quickly and accurately solve strategic business and information management problems. Headquartered in Darmstadt, Germany, SOFTWARE AG employs 2,800 people worldwide. ♦ This multinational organiza-

tion also has a strong presence in the United States, especially in the Washington area. SOFTWARE AG Americas is headquartered in Reston, Virginia, and half of SOFTWARE AG's nearly 800 employees in the United States work in the area.

"SOFTWARE AG has been serving the North American market since 1971, building our early reputation on industrial-strength databases," says Daniel F. Gillis, president and chief executive officer. "Our vision for the future is the concept of the enterprise information utility—providing unified information networks that provide users with access to the data they need, regardless of the complexity of the underlying technology infrastructure. There's a great demand to integrate business applications that run on older technology with the new wave

of Internet and intranet technology. SOFTWARE AG is well positioned to meet that demand."

THE HISTORY

SOFTWARE AG traces its beginnings to the AIV Institute, a German consultancy and contract

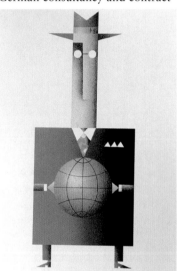

programming company that was active in the data processing market in the 1960s. As a subsidiary of the institute, SOFTWARE AG's initial mission was to create and market standard software products to complement AIV's developments. Because such products were still being offered as no-cost extras by hardware manufacturers, the company was unsuccessful at first.

For this reason, the company concentrated its entire efforts on one product, ADABAS, a full-scale production-oriented database management system.

Since those early days, SOFTWARE AG's products have continued to evolve according to the needs of its customers. Today SOFTWARE AG develops and markets three integrated product lines that run on platforms ranging from desktop to mainframe—

ADABAS for data management, NATURAL for application engineering, and ENTIRE for distributed computing solutions.

QUALITY SERVICE AND SUPPORT

SOFTWARE AG strives to "solve tomorrow's information needs today." In constantly changing business environments, SOFTWARE AG keeps its clients on the cutting edge by developing strategic mission-critical information access and management solutions. More important, SOFTWARE AG's industry-leading information technology, services, and support empower clients to meet business challenges—present and future.

To assure customers of competency in all strategic areas, SOFTWARE AG constantly forges alliances with key vendors of products and services that complement the company's own strengths. A growing list of companies reflects these strategic partnerships and alliances.

SOFTWARE AG enables companies to bridge the gap between information needs and technical possibility. Its reputation as a long-term independent business partner is earned every day in complex, mission-critical environments. Outstanding support and services are married to superior tools and technology to create total information solutions that are second to none.

AWARD-WINNING BUSINESS

SOFTWARE AG's innovations have not gone unnoticed. The company has earned the STAR Award for quality service and support, the *Business Week* Icon Award, the *Datamation* Quest award, *Datamation*'s Product of the Year award, and Midrange Systems' Buyers Choice Award.

In addition to these accolades, the company also recognizes its own employees for outstanding job performance and longevity with the company. The company gives Golden Circle awards for outstanding sales performance and recognizes employee tenure from the first week on the job. Gifts of escalating value are presented to employees to celebrate milestones in their employment with the company.

The President's Award is the most prestigious honor the company gives. It is given to the employee who has made a major contribution to the success of the company. The recipient is recognized for excelling at customer satisfaction, improving company operations and productivity, enhancing a company product or service set, and completing a feat that significantly affects the company.

The Profiles in Excellence awards recognize employees who have made significant contributions to the company. They consistently lend support, help, and guidance to customers and other employees and show evidence of outstanding dedication to their jobs and the company.

COMMUNITY COMMITMENT

SOFTWARE AG employees in the Washington area support a variety of charities and community causes. Among those consistently supported by the company are the American Cancer Society, the annual AIDS Walk in Washington to benefit the Whitman-Walker Clinic, and Reston Interfaith.

The beneficiaries of this community support have been appreciative. The American Cancer Society has commended SOFTWARE AG as a most valuable supporter and member of the American Cancer Society family, displaying dynamite leadership, energy, enthusiasm, and fundraising skills in every event in which it participates.

SOFTWARE AG is not only a good business partner in the Washington area, it also encourages good citizenship. And its employees rally to the call.

THE WATERGATE HOTEL HAS GAINED MUCH NAME RECOGNITION over the years by being part of the six-building complex that also houses the office space where the notorious Watergate break-in occurred in the 1970s. But, the hotel has also made a name for itself, building a reputation that stands on its own. It has been considered the site of Washington's most important social affairs for 30 years. ◆ With a luxurious

riverfront property that is a perfect setting for this grande dame of hotels in the nation's capital, The Watergate attracts business and leisure travelers who want to be pampered with perfection. Some 80 percent of the hotel's rooms have a view of the Potomac River, and the hotel is within walking distance of many of the city's attractions.

THE ROYAL TREATMENT

The Watergate offers elegant surroundings and gracious hospitality to all its guests. Antiques and fresh flowers accent the lobby and alcoves of the hotel, while The Watergate's 231 spacious rooms and suites offer amenities ranging from 24-hour room service to complimentary overnight shoe shine and limousine service to downtown. Every room contains a wet bar or full kitchen, and all the latest in communications equipment and connectability are available to the busy business traveler.

Watergate suites are decorated with fine antiques from the hotel's collection and are ideal for entertaining, private meetings, and extended stays. The magnificent Presidential Suites have one or two bedrooms, a living room, dining room, a full kitchen, and a wraparound balcony. The Diplomat Suites have a large separate bedroom, full kitchen, entertainment center, powder room, and master bath. Panoramic windows overlook the river and Georgetown. The Executive Suites feature living and dining areas that are separated from the bedroom by French doors. Most have balconies and many feature kitchenettes.

Even The Watergate's standard rooms are anything but standard. Amenities include fully stocked

minibars and complimentary bathrobes. Maid service is available twice daily, and newspapers are delivered to guests each day.

Aquarelle, the hotel's newest restaurant, offers diners a river view and an art-inspired atmosphere. Featuring sophisticated Euro-American cuisine prepared by critically acclaimed Executive Chef Robert Wiedmaier, Aquarelle has been cited by *Town & Country* magazine as the "Best New Bet" for dining out in D.C.

CATERING TO THE BUSINESS TRAVELER

The Watergate Hotel caters to the business traveler who wants calm, elegant surroundings. The staff reaches out to corporations to promote the hotel's relaxed atmosphere as a haven for business people who have been under stress. It's a place where business becomes a pleasure.

The hotel's business center provides telexing, telefaxing, copying, and typing services. There are also portable fax machines and telephones available.

The Watergate is known for hosting banquets and social occasions for five to 500 guests. More than 10,000 square feet of function space is conveniently located on one level. The permanent board room and private conference rooms range from 350 to more than 6,400 square feet. All meeting rooms can be configured to meet specific needs and are equipped with state-of-the-art audiovisual systems. The banquet staff customizes menus to meet every need and taste, and from the first planning session to the last detail, the experienced meeting and catering staff is committed to the utmost personal and professional service.

AND TO THE LEISURE TRAVELER

While many of The Watergate's guests are business and diplomatic travelers, the hotel also caters to leisure travelers. In addition to the wealth of tourist information provided by the hotel, guests are able to rent bicycles or obtain a lunch so they can picnic by the Potomac.

Located in the heart of Washington and just a few blocks from all the national landmarks, The Watergate supports many tourist activities. The hotel is only blocks from the Foggy Bottom Metro station, providing access to the city's subway system, and minutes away from National Airport, Union Station, the Capitol, the White House, and fashionable shops in Georgetown. It is also adjacent to the Kennedy Center for the Performing Arts.

Meanwhile, when it's time for an exercise break, the health club offers a competition-sized pool, jacuzzi, saunas, and a full range of exercise equipment. The facility helps guests maintain their fitness regimen during their stay at The Watergate. There are also spirited aerobics classes and guided walks along the Potomac scheduled throughout the day.

The Watergate Hotel is the place to see many of Washington's movers and shakers. The hotel's guest list has included political powerhouses such as heads of state from various countries, including Germany, Egypt, Japan, and Korea. There have been prominent cabinet-level guests from Israel, Pakistan, India, and Croatia. Former presidential candidate Steve Forbes has been a guest at the hotel, as has media mogul Ted Turner and his wife, actress Jane Fonda.

Other entertainers who have stayed at the hotel include Aretha Franklin, Placido Domingo, Richard Dreyfuss, Clint Eastwood, Tom Hanks, Paul Newman, Robert Redford, Stevie Wonder, Gloria Estefan, Mikhail Baryshnikov, and Kenny G.

But, you don't have to be rich or famous to be treated like a celebrity at The Watergate. Every guest is treated like someone special, giving the hotel a well-deserved reputation for luxury that will live for many years to come.

CLOCKWISE FROM TOP LEFT: THE WATERGATE IS KNOWN FOR HOSTING BANQUETS AND SOCIAL OCCASIONS FOR FIVE TO 500 GUESTS. THE BANQUET STAFF CUSTOMIZES MENUS TO MEET EVERY NEED AND TASTE, AND FROM THE FIRST PLANNING SESSION TO THE LAST DETAIL, THE EXPERIENCED MEETING AND CATERING STAFF IS COMMITTED TO THE UTMOST PERSONAL AND PROFESSIONAL SERVICE.

THE WATERGATE HOTEL'S AQUARELLE RESTAURANT OFFERS DINERS A RIVER VIEW AND AN ART-INSPIRED ATMOSPHERE.

EXECUTIVE CHEF ROBERT WIEDMAIER CREATES MASTERFUL EURO-AMERICAN DISHES FOR THE HOTEL'S ALL-DAY FINE DINING, AS WELL AS CATERING AND ROOM SERVICE.

WHUR-FM HAS BEEN INFORMING, EDUCATING, AND entertaining radio listeners in Washington for the past 25 years. The Howard University-owned and -operated station is one of only a handful of university-owned commercial radio stations in the United States. ◆ With a signal reaching from Baltimore, Maryland, to Richmond, Virginia,

WHUR is a major player in Washington's competitive radio market. Through the years, the station has had a strong impact in combining both contemporary and easy-listening music into sophisticated, urban programming. In 1976, WHUR initiated the renowned and often imitated Quiet Storm format—a progressive, easy-listening format rooted in mellow R&B music. The growth of a loyal local audience has prompted stations across the country to introduce this popular format into their own operations.

A WASHINGTON INSTITUTION

Originally having the call letters WTOP-FM, the station was given to Howard University in 1971 by *The Washington Post* during a period of divestiture. Since changing hands, the station adopted the call letters WHUR-FM and has evolved to become a successful, professional operation, as well as a profit center for the university.

WHUR employs nearly 40 people, and, although it provides paid internships for 20 students each semester, it does not rely heavily on students and interns. The station's management consists of an array of professional broadcasters who bring many years of experience from radio and television stations, newspapers, networks, and wire and rating services.

Preference for internships is given to Howard University students. WHUR has adopted the campus carrier station, WHBC—which only broadcasts on the Howard University campus—to find its most talented interns. The internships allow students to experience the radio industry while gaining important community service experience.

COMMUNITY COMMITMENT

WHUR's primary mission is to serve Washington's business and public communities,

CLOCKWISE FROM TOP: WHUR-FM HAS BEEN INFORMING, EDUCATING, AND ENTERTAINING RADIO LISTENERS IN WASHINGTON, FOR THE PAST 25 YEARS.

WHUR'S DIRECTOR OF CREATIVE SERVICES SCOTTY WEBB ASSISTS WITH THE PRODUCTION OF THE STATION'S SUCCESSFUL SHOWS.

THE STAFF AT WHUR-FM IS DEDICATED TO PROVIDING THE STATION'S LISTENERS WITH THE BEST IN URBAN PROGRAMMING.

and it has a long tradition of extensive community service. Each Saturday, the station hosts a community affairs program that features special segments of public service information. *WHUR Cityline* provides the community with job listings, public service announcements, entertainment news, and a host of other issues relevant to local residents. The station also delivers important news to the African-American community via *The Daily Drum*, which is broadcast Monday through Friday during prime-time hours.

In addition to its host of public service broadcasts and the donation of airtime to needy causes, the station staff actively participates in such community endeavors as Project Harvest, which collects more than $40,000 worth of food for the needy just before Thanksgiving.

WHUR has established its own volunteer group in order to better serve a greater number of projects. The organization, 96 Friends, is comprised of a core group of listeners who participate in community service and promotional events sponsored by the station. General Manager Millard J. Watkins III attributes the success of many of WHUR's community service programs to this dedicated group.

THE SOUND TO SUIT THE LISTENERS

WHUR's successful programming goes beyond the creation of the ever-popular Quiet Storm format. The station offers a variety of programs to appeal to the Washington community. Its mix of adult music ranges from a Caribbean show to gospel, jazz, rhythm and blues, progressive, and oldies.

When it comes to getting the African-American perspective on news, WHUR offers the most comprehensive coverage in the United States. WHUR's news team pro-

vides an in-depth analysis of international, national, and local news events through scheduled newscasts and interactive talk shows. In addition, the nationally syndicated *Tom Joyner Morning Show* originates at WHUR.

WHUR prides itself on being in touch with its listeners. To that end, the station performs extensive surveys and demographic studies to determine who its listeners are and what they want to hear. These studies have concluded that 60 percent of WHUR's listeners are African-American, with roughly the same percentage being women. Nearly three quarters of the station's listeners are between the ages of 25 and 54, more than 40 percent of whom live in Prince George's County. Nearly 95 percent have at least a high school education.

MAKING MUSIC A FINANCIAL SUCCESS

WHUR's sales department employs a dozen professionals who tailor the blocks of advertising time to the station's listener demographics. Watkins is proud of the fact that WHUR is able to help area businesses reach the local African-American community—a community with significant buying power—through on-air advertising.

"The purchasing power of African-Americans in the metropolitan Washington area is over $10 billion annually," explains Watkins. "WHUR-FM provides an excellent vehicle for businesses to expose their products and services to an efficient, upscale consumer base."

The station also employs a marketing team that provides in-depth station and market information to local and national advertisers, and provides research support and analysis from Arbitron, AID, Arbitrends, Qualitap, and Tapscan. With national sales representation from D&R Radio, WHUR's radio market is expanding rapidly, ensuring that its focus on the community and dedication to its listeners will continue well into the 21st century.

GENERAL MANAGER JIM WATKINS (LEFT) AND MEMBERS OF 96 FRIENDS UNLOAD VALENTINE'S DAY GIFTS FOR HOMELESS WOMEN.

OWNED AND OPERATED BY HOWARD UNIVERSITY, WHUR SPONSORS INTERNSHIPS THAT ALLOW STUDENTS TO EXPERIENCE THE RADIO INDUSTRY WHILE GAINING IMPORTANT COMMUNITY SERVICE EXPERIENCE.

Jerry's Ford, Inc.

Located in Annandale, Virginia, Jerry's Ford is a family-owned, family-friendly car dealership and service center. It was founded nearly a quarter-century ago by Jerry C. Cohen, who based the company on the philosophy of always putting the customer first. ◆ A lifelong resident of the Washington area, Cohen started his sales career in 1955 as a tagger with Handley Ford in Washington. He worked his way up to vice president and partner of that dealership before opening Jerry's Ford in 1973.

When Jerry's Ford opened, it was the largest one-site Ford dealership in the Washington area. The 8.5-acre lot opened with more than 350 cars and trucks in stock and another 550 on order. The 5,000-square-foot new-car showroom can accommodate 12 cars at one time, while the used-vehicle lot provides another 80,000 square feet of display space.

The service department opened with 45 service stalls and 15 more in the body shop. Both were supported by a completely stocked parts department with computerized inventory control. "We can provide every customer prompt and efficient diagnosis, maintenance, and repair service, whether his need is for routine mainte-

nance, complex diagnostic procedures, or major repair work," Cohen said the week the dealership opened.

Since the dealership's first day of business, Cohen's mission has always been to offer car and truck buyers the finest in sales and service. Today that philosophy is carried on by his son, Gary, who is general manager of Jerry's Ford.

Focusing on the Customer

Jerry's Ford tries to make the car-buying and -servicing experience as pleasant as possible for customers. For example, the dealership has a children's play area, equipped with videos and toys, so parents can conduct business without interruption. In addition, customers who bring laptops are able to use a lounge as a temporary office, and there are sales techniques in place to accommodate the buyers who don't want to negotiate price. "It's a non-confrontational selling style," Gary explains. "It's one price, no hassle."

Nearly a quarter-century ago, Jerry C. Cohen founded Jerry's Ford—a family-owned, family-friendly car dealership and service center—in Annandale, Virginia. He based the company on the philosophy of always putting the customer first (top).

When Jerry's Ford opened, it was the largest one-site Ford dealership in the Washington area, having an 8.5-acre lot with more than 350 cars and trucks in stock and another 550 on order (bottom).

THE 5,000-SQUARE-FOOT NEW-CAR
SHOWROOM AT JERRY'S FORD IS
CAPABLE OF ACCOMMODATING
12 CARS AT ONE TIME.

For years the service center has offered a 24-hour drop off service to those who cannot make it to the center during regular operating hours. Customers may leave their cars on the lot and their keys in a drop box after hours, so the problem can be addressed as soon as the center opens.

Jerry's Ford's philosophy of providing service after the sale is based on a belief that was articulated by its founder. "Selling a car is like getting engaged and then getting married," says Jerry Cohen. "After the marriage, a couple wants to stay together, and that's what [Jerry's Ford] wants to do. We want to marry all those customers and we want them to stay with us."

Jerry's Ford shows the same commitment to its employees as to its customers. Even today, a number of employees who were with the company on its first day of business continue to work at Jerry's. In addition, there is minimal employee turnover. Jerry once said, "I believe a big part of our success is that I've tried to surround myself with people who enjoy the business as much as I do."

AWARD-WINNING SERVICE

Jerry's Ford enters the 21st century with the latest technology to service vehicles. As automobile systems have become more complex, so has the detection of problems. But Jerry's is prepared for the challenge, drawing on a state-of-the-art diagnostic center.

If a problem cannot be diagnosed in the service center, for example, customers are sent home with a "flight recorder" that detects problems while away from the shop. In addition, if a local service representative is unable to solve a problem, he is able to plug in electronically to Ford's service center for additional assistance.

Such service has earned Jerry's a rich history as an award-winning dealership and service center. The honors received over the years have included a rating of superior service by an independent consumer's group, an American Automobile Association (AAA) approval rating, the Ford Motor Company's Gold Medallion Award for parts and service, and Ford's Distinguished Achievement award.

Nominated for the award by the Automobile Trade Association of the National Capital Area, Jerry was honored in 1989 as a *Time* Magazine Quality Dealer at the National Automobile Dealers Association (NADA) convention in New Orleans. The award is given to a new-car dealer for "exceptional performance in (his dealership) combined with distinguished community service." *Time* magazine sponsors the quality dealer award in cooperation with NADA, and the 67 winners across the nation in 1989 were chosen by faculty members of the University of Michigan's Graduate School of Business Administration.

But Jerry Cohen's greatest reward is doing something he loves. He says, "As long as you enjoy doing this, it's fun. You can make money, have fun, and, at the same time, it's not a chore."

Ideally located in historic Foggy Bottom—one of Washington's finest neighborhoods—One Washington Circle Hotel offers a front row seat to a city brimming with excitement. This full-service hotel offers suites with European flair, charm, warmth, and what General Manager Saleem Malik calls a "home-away-from-home feeling." ♦ The One Washington Circle Hotel caters to government, corporate, and leisure travelers, and all receive a personal

level of service and "welcome home" treatment from the minute they walk into the lobby. Each of the 151 luxury suites contains a fully equipped gourmet kitchen stocked with fresh coffee beans, a grinder, and a coffeemaker.

ELEGANT AMBIENCE

Elegance defines a visitor's stay at the One Washington Circle Hotel. The establishment takes pride in making each traveler's stay as comfortable as possible with a high degree of personal service by its attentive and caring staff. The hotel's luxurious sur-

roundings include its two-level lobby with highly polished wood-paneled walls, modern art, and plush seating areas. Guests are afforded a quiet, private, and spacious environment.

The staff stresses guest services, providing visitors with all the comforts of home and none of the responsibilities, thus making the hotel conducive to both long- and short-term stays.

In addition to the suites, the hotel offers superior meeting accommodations. Its creative, professional staff can assist meeting planners in the design

of everything from the menu to the mood. Six meeting rooms are available that can accommodate from 10 to 125 attendees.

Guests of the One Washington Circle Hotel have easy access to fine dining at one of Washington's premier restaurants, the West End Cafe, located inside the hotel. Washington's most discerning food critics rave about the West End Cafe's trend-setting American cooking. The restaurant's lively, unpretentious style makes it the ideal setting for lingering over creative dishes and enjoying spirited conversation under the Garden Room's greenhouse roof. For informal socializing, guests can settle into a cozy corner of the Piano Room and let the sounds of jazz simmer their senses.

The One Washington Circle Hotel's close proximity to numerous tourist attractions makes it the perfect place to stay while taking in the sights of the capital city. The hotel is located just blocks from the Foggy Bottom and Farragut North metro stops, making touring simple for visitors who prefer to leave the driving to the city's mass transit system. The hotel is also close to such attractions as the White House, Georgetown, national monuments and memorials, the Smithsonian, the National Gallery of Art, and the Kennedy Center.

With all the comforts of home and easy access to destinations around Washington, it is not surprising that the hotel boasts a large amount of repeat business. "Once visitors have experienced this hotel," explains Malik, "they return again and again."

CLOCKWISE FROM TOP: GUESTS OF THE ONE WASHINGTON CIRCLE HOTEL HAVE EASY ACCESS TO FINE DINING AT ONE OF WASHINGTON'S PREMIER RESTAURANTS, THE WEST END CAFE, LOCATED INSIDE THE HOTEL.

THE ONE WASHINGTON CIRCLE HOTEL CATERS TO GOVERNMENT, CORPORATE, AND LEISURE TRAVELERS, AND ALL RECEIVE A PERSONAL LEVEL OF SERVICE AND "WELCOME HOME" TREATMENT FROM THE MINUTE THEY WALK INTO THE LOBBY.

EACH OF THE 151 LUXURY SUITES CONTAINS A FULLY EQUIPPED GOURMET KITCHEN STOCKED WITH FRESH COFFEE BEANS, A GRINDER, AND A COFFEEMAKER.

Feddeman & Company, P.C.

EDDEMAN & COMPANY, P.C. (F&Co.) HAS CARVED OUT ITS NICHE BY adhering to its mission to provide the best accounting, auditing, tax, and consulting services available to associations and not-for-profits with unparalleled consistency, timeliness, and professionalism. ◆ F&Co. is truly unique. Its expertise in providing not-for-profits with specialized services, accessibility to pertinent resources, flexibility, and responsiveness—

delivered with speed, efficiency, and personal attention—is unparalleled. F&Co.'s publications state: "We set excellence as our standard throughout our staffing and rendering of services to our clients."

THE ENTREPRENEURIAL SPIRIT

W. Kent Feddeman formed the accounting firm in 1979, detecting a need among not-for-profits for more personal, customized service. Today, F&Co. serves more associations than any other CPA firm in the Washington metropolitan area. By choosing a specialty, the firm has positioned itself as a leader in serving associations.

Feddeman searches for employees who have a rapport with people and are enthusiastic about their work. Business development and creativity are encouraged. Above all, providing the best service possible remains the primary focus for all staff members.

Feddeman notes that the staff is the backbone of Feddeman & Company. He explains, "Our principal asset is our experienced and dedicated staff. We are aggressive and proactive in our service, creative and spirited, and committed to providing the highest level of quality in our work while serving not-for-profit organizations exclusively. Our professional and support staff enthusiastically subscribe to our mission."

FORWARD THINKING

In the latter half of the 1990s, outsourcing of the accounting function makes sense for many nonprofits. F&Co. has seen tre-

ROBERT VISSER

mendous growth in this area, and Feddeman predicts that F&Co. will continue to grow along these lines, while maintaining its mission of providing the best services to associations and nonprofits in the Washington metropolitan area.

STRATEGICALY LOCATED IN ALEXANDRIA, VIRGINIA, FEDDEMAN & COMPANY SERVES CLIENTS THROUGHOUT THE ENTIRE WASHINGTON METROPOLITAN AREA (TOP).

FEDDEMAN & COMPANY'S DIRECTORS ARE (FROM LEFT) NATHANIAL T. BARTHOLOMEW, CPA; JOSEPH M. KOTWICKI, CPA; W. KENT FEDDEMAN, CPA; J. ANDREW SMITH, CPA; AND CHERYL L. JORDAN, CPA (BOTTOM).

ROBERT VISSER

THE LARGEST INDEPENDENT PROFESSIONAL SERVICES COMPANY IN the world, Electronic Data Systems Corporation (EDS) is a leader in applying information services to meet the needs of businesses, industries, and governments around the globe. The company offers a broad range of performance-based information management services such as consulting; systems development, integration, and management;

telecommunications; hardware and software integration; networking; reengineering; and process management.

Headquartered in Plano, Texas, EDS received its independence in a 1996 spin-off from General Motors Corporation. The company maintains offices in 42 countries and has a team of more than 100,000 (including 4,000 in the Washington, D.C., area) employees serving a 9,000-plus customer base.

GOVERNMENT SERVICES GROUP

The Government Services Group (GSG) is based at EDS' eastern region headquarters in Herndon, Virginia. Dedicated to helping all levels of government manage costs and improve public service, GSG employs more than 3,300 people in management, marketing and sales, technical support, and account operations worldwide.

GSG offers a broad range of performance-based information management services. EDS' government business worldwide produces approximately 15 percent of the corporation's revenues.

The company entered the state government marketplace in the mid-1960s, expanded its information services into the federal government arena during the 1970s, and added local government business in the late 1980s. Since then, GSG has grown to become a global leader in developing and applying information services for the benefit of enterprises and individuals around the globe.

GSG works with U.S. government agencies around the world in the areas of immigration, law enforcement, health care management, scientific data tracking, housing loans, transportation systems, agricultural commodities management, aviation, personnel management, traffic management and enforcement operations, human services, electronic commerce, environmental regulation systems, public safety, education, and small-business development. EDS also serves the U.S. Department of Defense and other agencies worldwide with information management products and services to support such vital areas as defense systems reengineering; strategic planning; logistics; human resources; indefinite

CLOCKWISE FROM TOP: EDS' EASTERN REGION HEADQUARTERS BUILDING IN HERNDON, VIRGINIA, IS HOME TO THE GOVERNMENT SERVICES GROUP (GSG).

EDS SUPPORTS THE *Information Age* EXHIBIT IT CO-FOUNDED AT THE SMITHSONIAN INSTITUTION'S NATIONAL MUSEUM OF AMERICAN HISTORY IN WASHINGTON, D.C. THE 12,000-SQUARE-FOOT DISPLAY IS NOT ONLY AN ASSEMBLAGE OF COMMUNICATIONS AND COMPUTER ARTIFACTS SINCE THE TIME OF THE TELEGRAPH, IT IS ALSO A SHOWCASE OF THE LATEST ADVANCES IN INFORMATION TECHNOLOGY (IT).

THE LARGEST INDEPENDENT PROFESSIONAL SERVICES COMPANY IN THE WORLD, EDS IS A LEADER IN APPLYING INFORMATION SERVICES TO MEET THE NEEDS OF BUSINESSES, INDUSTRIES, AND GOVERNMENTS AROUND THE GLOBE.

delivery/indefinite quantity (ID/IQ) and governmentwide agency contracts (GWAC) programs; intelligence; finance; electronic commerce/ electronic data interchange (EC/ EDI); and command and control operations.

COMMUNITY OUTREACH

Every year, EDS employees in the Washington area spend thousands of hours volunteering in their communities. They participate in the company's Global Volunteer Day each fall, working on such projects as refurbishing and repairing houses for the needy and helping underprivileged children and senior citizens.

EDS volunteers also are involved in projects to aid Washington-area schools, such as Education Outreach, an employee volunteer-based school partnership program. The company supports education to help develop students into members of a workforce that can meet the business needs and technical challenges of the coming century. Through the Education Outreach program, EDS employees collaborate with school staff to set partnership goals that match the needs of each school and the skills of the company's volunteers.

Volunteers for Education Outreach work as student tutors and mentors; help develop curricula; organize computer clubs; serve as career speakers; coordinate field trips and special programs;

provide technology consulting, hardware, services, and training to students and teachers; and join with students in a multitude of community service projects. The program has received community recognition for its superior contribution to education.

Other EDS-sponsored education initiatives include the Technology Grant program, which gives monetary awards to elementary teachers around the world to fund their proposals for using technology to enhance classroom learning, and a fund-raising campaign for the Challenger Learning Center, which was founded by the families of the *Challenger* astronauts as a living memorial to the crew. The center's program is designed to motivate young students to study science and mathematics through a curriculum that includes simulated space missions that take place at 29 locations across the country.

EDS also supports the *Information Age* exhibit it founded at the Smithsonian Institution in Washington. The 12,000-square-foot display is an assemblage of communications and computer artifacts since the time of the telegraph, and a showcase of the latest advances in information technology (IT).

THE JASON PROJECT

The company is the founding sponsor and technology

provider for the annual JASON Project, world renowned for its use of telepresence technology to bring the expedition to more than 500,000 students each year. The JASON Project is the brainchild of Dr. Robert Ballard, who discovered the RMS *Titanic* wreckage. His vision is to use technology to share the thrill of discovery with young minds, igniting new enthusiasm for science. EDS' technological support and commitment to the project help make the vision a reality for young students everywhere.

Each year since 1989, the project has taken students on expeditions around the world. From a network of sites in the United States, England, Mexico, and Bermuda, the students have followed scientists to such places as the Galápagos Islands, Belize, Hawaii, and the floor of the Mediterranean Sea. They've studied marine life, sunken ships, a tropical rain forest, a coral reef, birds, animals, and volcanoes.

EDS' support of educational programs that encourage an interest in mathematics and science ultimately benefits the company. In an increasingly competitive industry where a growing number of high-tech companies are trying to attract the best and the brightest, EDS is making the pool of talent a little bigger.

EDS VOLUNTEERS ARE INVOLVED IN PROJECTS TO AID WASHINGTON, D.C.,-AREA SCHOOLS, SUCH AS EDUCATION OUTREACH, AN EMPLOYEE VOLUNTEER-BASED SCHOOL PARTNERSHIP PROGRAM. THE COMPANY SUPPORTS EDUCATION TO HELP DEVELOP STUDENTS INTO MEMBERS OF A WORKFORCE THAT CAN MEET THE BUSINESS NEEDS AND TECHNICAL CHALLENGES OF THE COMING CENTURY.

THE FRED EZRA COMPANY

T HOSE SEEKING OFFICE SPACE IN THE WASHINGTON AREA TURN TO The Fred Ezra Company. Established in 1980, Ezra has become one of the leading commercial real estate firms in the nation, specializing in tenant representation. Built on knowledge, experience, and uncompromising integrity, the firm has always set the highest standard of excellence in serving its clients. ♦ A full-service firm, Ezra helps its clients find

EZRA'S TEAM IS AVAILABLE TO EVALUATE AND SECURE COMMERCIAL REAL ESTATE; PROVIDE A HOST OF PROJECT MANAGEMENT AND CONSTRUCTION MANAGEMENT SERVICES TO CREATE A DESIRED WORK ENVIRONMENT; AND MONITOR AND MANAGE THE MOVE, AS WELL AS SUPPLY LEASE ADMINISTRATION AND LITIGATION SUPPORT SERVICES DURING THE TERM OF THE LEASE (RIGHT).

real estate, then negotiates the deal, manages the project, and provides ongoing service and support throughout the term of a lease. With offices in Bethesda, Maryland; Washington, D.C.; and McLean, Virginia, the firm serves nearly 250 clients a year in the Washington metropolitan area and across the nation.

Integrity is a key component of Ezra's business philosophy. Unlike most firms, which primarily represent the interest of landlords, Ezra's allegiance is exclusively with tenants. The firm avoids all conflicts of interest created when representing both landlords and tenants. Ezra's philosophy is that a broker that serves both sides facilitates a deal rather than negotiates one, depriving the tenant of receiving the best possible deal. Ezra, on the other hand, guarantees the best terms and conditions for its client. The firm accomplishes this through its team of some of the most skilled, aggressive negotiators in the business. The integrity of its staff is part of Ezra's growing national reputation and has always been a draw for local clients.

Ezra remains available to a client long after a lease is signed. The firm takes great pride in the large number of clients that have returned to the firm for its ability to design and negotiate creative deal structures. Each package is designed for a specific client, so the firm's expertise is used to customize terms that best suit the needs of each client.

QUALITY STAFF

M embers of The Fred Ezra Company are committed to

excellence in the service of their clients. They are high-energy, seasoned professionals with one mission: To provide their clients with the highest-quality service.

Ezra's highly qualified brokers and support staff don't let grass grow under their feet. They are well trained, and they continue to stay on top of their field by taking advantage of a host of continuing education opportunities offered by the firm. As part of the total quality management philosophy, training focuses on many different topics, ranging from negotiation skills to project management classes. Staying abreast of business developments and understanding clients' needs are priorities.

THE FUTURE

E zra now represents corporate clients with nationwide requirements. The Corporate Services Group provides the same superior representation for clients through-

out the country that it has been providing in the Washington area since 1980. The company utilizes existing technology and looks for new developments in an effort to remain on the cutting edge of tenant opportunities.

The Ezra team is also expanding its range of services. Ezra is available to evaluate and secure commercial real estate; provide a host of project management and construction management services; monitor and manage the tenant's move; and supply tenant lease management and litigation support services.

The Fred Ezra Company's services are geared to meet today's changing market requirements and to serve the sophisticated technical needs of a variety of clients. The Ezra Team is dedicated to ensuring that its clients achieve an office environment that is revenue enhancing while integrating their real estate and organizational goals.

BUILT ON KNOWLEDGE, EXPERIENCE, AND UNCOMPROMISING INTEGRITY, THE FIRM HAS ALWAYS SET THE HIGHEST STANDARD OF EXCELLENCE IN SERVING ITS CLIENTS.

As THE CONSERVATIVE VOICE OF THE NATION'S CAPITAL, *The Washington Times*, with a circulation of 100,000, is widely quoted by news organizations and news makers around the world. Established in 1982 by News World Communications, the *Times* hit the newsstands nine months after the *Washington Star* shut its doors in 1981, again making the nation's capital a two-newspaper town.

From the beginning, the *Times* has brought a fresh and fearless approach to journalism. The paper is clear about where it stands and where it is going, all the while striving to bring facts to light and values into focus. Although it is not a Republican publication, the *Times* proudly accepts the label of having a conservative view, with the goal of seeking to balance the liberal slant found in many publications today.

The acceptance of the lively newspaper, which is responsive to the interests and lifestyles of its readers, is evident by its ever expanding circulation. According to Wesley Pruden, editor in chief, "When *The Washington Times* speaks, the world listens. Because we get picked up by the wire services, we go all over the world."

JOURNALISTIC EXCELLENCE

The 800 employees at *The Washington Times* are dedicated to excellence and take pride in setting industry standards. Suspicious of the conventional wisdom and current consensus, *Times* reporters make their own calls and confirm every story. They strive to provide a reality check.

The Washington Times and its staff have been recognized and rewarded for their efforts. The newspaper has received hundreds of prestigious awards for its editorial, business, sports, and investigative reporting, as well as accolades for its design and photography. Of the nearly 250 journalists who contribute to the publication, many have won some of the industry's highest honors.

THE WASHINGTON TIMES ON-LINE

In an attempt to remain on the cutting edge of technology, *The Washington Times* also has an electronic Internet edition that features news selections, photographs, editorials, columns, and other materials taken from the day's printed edition. Reflecting the political nature of the nation's capital, the Times On-Line emphasizes political coverage and can be found at http://www.washtimes.com.

The electronic edition of the *Times* is further evidence of one of the most technically advanced newsrooms and press facilities in the business. The *Times* is assured of a steady future in Washington and around the world.

ESTABLISHED IN 1982, *The Washington Times* BRINGS BALANCED NEWS COVERAGE TO THE NATION'S CAPITAL.

KAISER FOUNDATION HEALTH PLAN OF THE MID-ATLANTIC STATES, PART of the Kaiser Permanente Medical Care Program, is a nonprofit, prepaid group practice serving residents of Maryland, Virginia, and the District of Columbia. The Mid-Atlantic Permanente Medical Group provides or arranges care for the more than 530,000 members of Kaiser Permanente. ◆ Permanente was established in the mid-Atlantic states area in

1980, when Kaiser Permanente assumed responsibility for the Georgetown University Community Health Plan. Kaiser Permanente has 22 medical centers, two mental health centers, an imaging center, and several ancillary facilities that provide services to its members. The health plan also has developed successful partnerships with area hospitals, such as Holy Cross Hospital, INOVA Fairfax Hospital, and the Washington Hospital Center.

Nationally, the Kaiser Permanente Medical Care Program provides health care services to 7.9 million members in 18 states and the District of Columbia.

A SOLID REPUTATION FOR QUALITY AND MEMBER SATISFACTION

Kaiser Permanente has reason to be proud of its performance and record in the Middle Atlantic states. It was awarded the highest possible level of accreditation by the National Committee for Quality Assurance for having

CLOCKWISE FROM TOP: KAISER PERMANENTE BELIEVES IN PROVIDING ITS MEMBERS WITH CONVENIENCE. ITS 22 MEDICAL CENTERS OFFER MANY SERVICES UNDER ONE ROOF, INCLUDING PRIMARY AND SPECIALTY CARE, LAB, RADIOLOGY, VISION SERVICES, PHARMACY, AND MORE.

EARLY PRENATAL CARE IS JUST ONE WAY KAISER PERMANENTE FOCUSES ON PREVENTION.

Professor Bodywise IS KAISER PERMANENTE'S EDUCATIONAL THEATER PLAY THAT TEACHES CHILDREN HEALTH AND SAFETY HABITS.

excellent programs in continuous quality improvement, physician credentialing, members' rights and responsibilities, preventive health services, utilization management, and medical records. The health plan continually works on meeting customers' expectations on quality, as well as employers' needs for new products. The health plan consistently receives high ratings in member satisfaction from external surveys.

WORKING HARD TO MAINTAIN GOOD HEALTH

Kaiser Permanente believes that health maintenance and prevention are vital to the well-being of its members and to the company's health plan. In theory and in practice, Kaiser Permanente works hard to maintain a person's good health. They do this by providing high-quality health care that's personable, affordable, and patient focused. The company's health

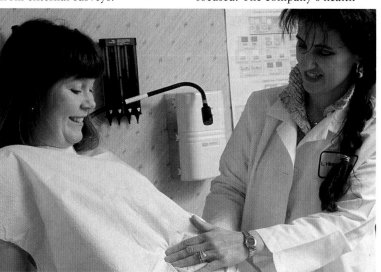

plan offers a wide range of services, including primary and specialty care, ambulatory surgery, laboratory, radiology, physical therapy, pharmacy, optical, and more.

The company is proud of its many programs that focus on keeping members healthy. For example, Kaiser Permanente has a Tender Loving Care Program that's designed to increase the incidence of full-term deliveries. All pregnant women are screened for risk factors that may result in premature birth. High-risk patients are followed closely throughout their pregnancy. Patients also receive education and individualized counseling about how to prevent preterm labor. This kind of early intervention and prenatal care prevents a host of problems during pregnancy and results in healthier, full-term babies. Other successful programs include Kaiser Permanente's Self-Care Program—which helps members take a more active, informed role in their health care—and its programs on asthma, hypertension, diabetes, and more.

A Partnership That Makes a Difference

Kaiser Permanente is a successful partnership between medicine and management. The medical group focuses on providing care to members while management focuses on the day-to-day, administrative aspects of the business. In this structure, there's an emphasis on physician responsibility. Kaiser Permanente doctors make all medical decisions and determine medical policy.

The medical group has more than 550 physicians who represent an even mix of primary and specialty care. Physicians must be board certified or board eligible when they join Kaiser Permanente. If they are eligible when they are hired, they must achieve certification within four years. While the national average for board-certi-

fied physicians is only 60 percent, more than 96 percent of Kaiser Permanente physicians are board certified.

The mid-Atlantic area has some unique health care needs, which the company's health plan strives to meet. For example, because the area has a large Hispanic population, Kaiser Permanente employs bilingual physicians. It also has ongoing cultural diversity programs to help staff and physicians understand better the health care needs in this market.

More than 3,500 well-trained, committed, and caring staff members support the doctors in health care delivery. Kaiser Permanente is proud of the dedication and rich diversity of its employee population. The company invests in its staff through ongoing training and development programs.

Kaiser Permanente is a nonprofit organization that is committed to the health and well-being of its communities. Many of its staff and physicians live and volunteer in the diverse communities in which the company serves. Kaiser Permanente provides care to underserved children and families through dues subsidy programs and a variety of public/private partnerships. The organization also sponsors the Building Hope Initiative, which focuses on youth violence prevention through an annual conference, workshops, a newsletter, a grants program, and an interactive theater production—called RAVES (Real Alternatives to Violence for Every Student)—that teaches skills in conflict resolution and anger management.

Kaiser Permanente also offers free, award-winning educational theater programs. The popular theater productions focus on health and safety habits for younger children, AIDS education, and the communication challenges between parents and teens.

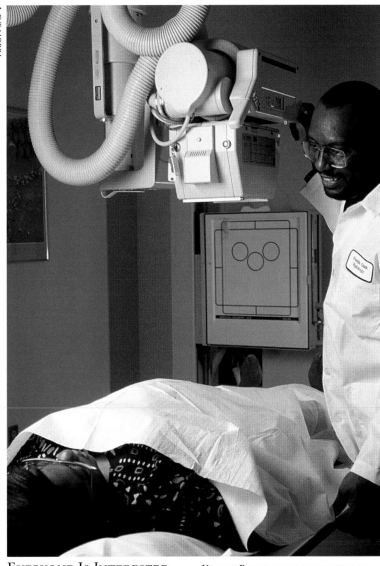

EVE MORRA

Everyone Is Interested in the Bottom Line

For Kaiser Permanente—an organization with a conscience—a healthy bottom line is accomplished with a commitment to responsible stewardship of the members' premiums. The company reinvests its income in its members through having the latest technology and the most advanced health care regimens and programs that help individuals lead safe, healthy, and more fulfilling lives. In an era of rapid change and volatility in the health care field, Kaiser Permanente's long history of financial stability and fiscal prudence is reassuring to members and the communities they serve.

KAISER PERMANENTE REINVESTS IN ITS MEMBERS BY USING THE LATEST, MOST SOPHISTICATED TECHNOLOGY.

BEST SOFTWARE, INC.

THE GREATEST TESTAMENT TO THE SUCCESS OF BEST SOFTWARE, Inc. is the number of products that bear the Best name. The company provides a broad range of desktop business solutions software for midsize businesses worldwide. Founded in 1982 by Chairman Jim Petersen, Best is the leader in desktop human resource, payroll, and fixed asset management solutions for more than 40,000 businesses throughout

North America.

The company, which introduced a Microsoft Windows-based fixed asset system, has found a niche among the companies it serves. Petersen credits his customers with making Best the top name in fixed asset solutions. "We have earned their trust for reliability, rich functionality, and, especially, ease of use," Petersen explains. "In fact, throughout the United States, three out of every five PC-based fixed asset systems are from Best, and the majority of the Big Six and many regional firms rely on Best as their preferred provider of fixed asset solutions."

RECOGNIZED EXPERIENCE

Best concentrates on providing powerful, finely tuned PC software expressly designed to help companies manage the intricacies of legislative and regulatory requirements that continually plague the corporate financial picture. These include regulatory changes to employee hiring practices, new payroll reporting rules, and Internal Revenue Service reporting changes affecting fixed asset depreciation requirements.

It is the company's focus on the midsize company that attracted Best's president and chief executive officer, Tim Davenport, to the com-

pany. "I became excited about the upside of trying to serve the middle market," explains Davenport. "The more I learned about Best, I saw that it had served its market well for 10 years, and that over the next four or five years, there was a chance for expansion."

A DIVERSE ARRAY OF PRODUCTS

Best's software is divided into two lines: FAS software for fixed asset management and the Abra products group for human resources and payroll. The fixed asset management division is located in Reston, Virginia, while

BEST'S INDUSTRY-LEADING FAS LINE OF FIXED ASSET MANAGEMENT SOFTWARE AND ITS ABRA LINE OF AWARD-WINNING HUMAN RESOURCE AND PAYROLL SOFTWARE ARE CONSISTENTLY RANKED IN THE TOP 100 SOFTWARE PRODUCTS BY *Accounting Today.*

the human resources and payroll solutions group is based in St. Petersburg, Florida.

The FAS product line includes FAS for Windows, FAS Encore!, FASTrack for Windows, FAS2000, and FAS1000. Add-on modules are ImportPlus—which imports fixed asset information from Lotus, Symphony, or Excel—and FAS Report Writer for Windows. The company has also developed custom linking software that will allow seamless transfer of information to and from a customer's accounting system to Best's products.

The Abra products include Abra HR for Windows, Abra Applicant for Windows, and Abra Payroll for Windows. Add-on modules include Abra Attendance for Windows, Abra Toolkit for Windows, Abra Link for Windows, Abra Train for Windows, and Abra Multi-Site Consolidation for Windows.

QUALITY SERVICE AND SUPPORT

Best backs every program with expert service and support. In fact, quality customer support is the hallmark of Best Software.

The FAS SupportPlus® service includes an array of privileges, discounts, and value-added benefits. These include toll-free telephone support, timely updates to changes in tax laws, a free newsletter subscription, discounts on new products and professional seminars, a convenient fax service to exchange technical questions with the Customer Service Center, and access to the on-line "Members Lounge."

The Abra technical support and product update service includes toll-free telephone support, fax and E-mail access to the Abra Products Group Technical Support, full access to the Abra Products Group Bulletin Board System, product updates and upgrades, and newsletters with helpful tips on using Abra products.

BEST PRESIDENT AND CEO TIM DAVENPORT IS RESPONSIBLE FOR GUIDING THE CREATION OF NEW PRODUCTS AND MANAGING THE GROWTH OF BEST SOFTWARE IN BOTH INTERNATIONAL AND DOMESTIC MARKETS.

CHAIRMAN JIM PETERSEN FOUNDED BEST SOFTWARE IN 1982. TODAY, IT IS THE LEADER IN DESKTOP HUMAN RESOURCE, PAYROLL, AND FIXED ASSET MANAGEMENT SOLUTIONS FOR MORE THAN 40,000 BUSINESSES THROUGHOUT NORTH AMERICA.

With a 15-year heritage in PC software, Best truly stands for the mark of experience. The firm delivers expert solutions that make sense, make jobs easier, and make its clients' most precious resources perform better. Best Software prides itself on being the best in the business and recruits the best software engineers in the industry in order to always be on the cutting edge of technology. "Managing today's financial office brings new complexities every day," acknowledges Petersen. Yet he says his company is ready to meet that challenge. "I'm confident we have the right

expertise and the right technology to help our customers, today and in the years to come."

Best is consistently recognized by major industry accounting and software publications. The company has been listed as one of *Accounting Today*'s Top 100 Accounting Software Companies, *Computer Reseller News*' Top 50 Independent Software Companies, and *PC Magazine*'s Top 200 Players in the PC Industry.

"I'm very proud of what we've accomplished," concludes Petersen. "I'm even more excited about where we're headed."

BORN AS A SPIN-OFF OF THE ENGINEERING SERVICES FIRM NETWORK Solutions, NetCom Solutions International, Inc. has built its own legacy over the past 15 years as a company that helps its clients create and improve user productivity through the most efficient use of voice and data communications networks. ♦ "NetCom Solutions started with a legacy of excellence for meeting and exceeding our customers'

quality requirements," according to Emmit J. McHenry, president and chief executive officer. "Our client approach is to design processes to meet the requirements, as well as providing staff to implement the requirements and review the outcome with our client-partner. We have learned over time that the best customer-service provider relationships occur when the service provider and service recipient share mutual understanding and commitment to work together as partners."

Based in Herndon, Virginia, NetCom Solutions has service locations across the United States and its territories. A nationwide staff of engineers and network field technicians, who support diverse network and telecommunications equipment, are deployed from NetCom Solutions' National Response Center in Oklahoma City. A design center serves domestic and international partners and clients with state-of-the-art technology solutions. In addition, NetCom Solutions provides a help desk 24 hours a day, seven days a week.

The company also has a growing international presence. Currently, NetCom Solutions has strategic partners in South Africa, Zimbabwe, Kenya, Côte d'Ivoire, and Ethiopia, and is investigating additional partnerships throughout Africa.

FOUNDING PRINCIPLES

NetCom Solutions was founded on five basic principles: integrity, quality, employee satisfaction, an open communication culture, and profitability. These principles are shared with

everyone inside and outside the company, so everyone understands how NetCom Solutions operates.

NetCom Solutions stresses integrity in all business relationships, maintaining that honesty is, and will be, the basis for trust in all dealings with those inside and outside the company. No agreements are made without having first established that the company is able and willing to honor the terms of the agreement.

The company is committed to maintaining outstanding quality in all its products and services, and promises to deliver the highest quality possible within the customer's constraints of cost and

schedule. At NetCom Solutions, quality is measured by how well the company's services and products help customers achieve their purposes.

The expertise and commitment of NetCom Solutions' employees are its greatest assets. The company strives to be an employer of choice by providing fair and reasonable compensation, opportunities for career development, a role in the participative management of the company, and a commitment to view each employee as a whole person.

NetCom Solutions encourages a free flow of communications between customers, management,

EMMIT J. MCHENRY, PRESIDENT AND CHIEF EXECUTIVE OFFICER OF NETCOM SOLUTIONS INTERNATIONAL, INC.

and all employees. Each person's perspective is a resource for helping the company grow and prosper. Toward this end, each employee is continually reminded to support or clarify issues about the company; assume personal responsibility when a problem arises in order that the problem may be solved efficiently; strive for clarity in all agreements; communicate with concerned parties regarding potential broken agreements as soon as possible to avoid misunderstandings and possible risks for others; and revise decisions without faultfinding.

The achievement of fair and reasonable profit is the basis for continuous improvement in the services NetCom Solutions provides to its customers, the environment provided for employees, and the attainment of an overall goal. It is a measure of the company's success in being a premier service provider to its customers.

ONE-STOP SHOPPING

Positioned for the next century as a premier provider of applied networking communications services and technology, the emphasis at NetCom Solutions is on mastery. A provider of network communications engineering, technical field services, provisioning, and materials management support, the company focuses on state-of-the-art networked communications solutions. NetCom Solutions offers design, installation, integration, and maintenance services, supporting its clients and partners around the world.

The company's core competencies include engineering design, integration and installation of hardware and software, value-added distribution, full-service network maintenance, and depot repair and refurbishment. There's also a focus on wireless multimedia wide-area network communication system design and implementation in developing countries.

"NetCom Solutions is on a continuing quest to create an

entrepreneurial culture of people committed to mastering the delivery of network engineering services and technology in support of our client-partners," says McHenry. "We seek to enhance the already outstanding quality of products and services we provide. It is our way of winning trust."

NetCom Solutions is a business built around continuous development of its staff. Recruiting people with exceptional technical expertise, the firm also seeks those with an entrepreneurial spirit. Those who become a part of this professional "family" are mentored and coached; continuing educa-

tion isn't just encouraged, it's required. "The practice of mastery is a becoming process," explains McHenry. "It starts with an unwavering vision of the possible and focuses on continuous improvement."

Because NetCom Solutions is committed to mastery in its industry, the company strives to excel in customer satisfaction in all aspects of product delivery and service—a logical extension of its founding management principles and a critical part of its identity. Quality service is "the difference that will make the difference" for NetCom Solutions.

CLOCKWISE FROM TOP: NETCOM SOLUTIONS IS HEADQUARTERED IN HERNDON, VIRGINIA.

THE INTEGRATION CENTER BRINGS HARDWARE AND SOFTWARE TOGETHER TO OFFER SOLUTIONS.

ENGINEERS AND NETWORK FIELD TECHNICIANS ARE DEPLOYED FROM THE NATIONAL RESPONSE CENTER.

THE NETWORK OPERATIONS CENTER IS HOUSED IN HERNDON, VIRGINIA.

Experience equals quality, and Horizon Data Corporation is positioned to be the quality company for the 21st century. The company's prime business areas of expertise include information technology networks and communications, application software development, data center management and operations, and health care systems. ◆ For over a decade, Horizon Data Corporation (HDC) has supplied information technology

solutions to commercial and federal clients. Founded in 1983, HDC now provides a full spectrum of services in the information technology field.

Headquartered in Reston, Virginia, HDC is strategically located less than 20 miles from Capitol Hill—just over six miles from Dulles International Airport—and manages a state-of-the-art computer center just two miles from headquarters. HDC was founded by José R. Rivera and David E. Walp, businessmen with talent and integrity. Their leadership and dedication continue to grow HDC into an organization spanning the east, west, and southern coasts of the United States.

The federal government comprises approximately half of the company's client base, with the other half being divided between health care and commercial. Through carefully targeted expansion, the company has successfully leveraged its expertise and experience into the three prime markets as few young companies are able to do.

HDC IS LOCATED STRATEGICALLY IN THE MIDDLE OF THE HUB ALONG THE DULLES TECHNOLOGY CORRIDOR AND THE NATION'S CAPITAL.

DAVID E. WALP, CO-FOUNDER (LEFT), AND JOSÉ R. RIVERA, FOUNDER, ARE THE SUCCESSFUL CO-OWNERS OF HORIZON DATA CORPORATION.

A SUCCESS STORY

HDC credits its rapid growth to its ability to satisfy customer needs in a straightforward and cost-effective manner. The company maintains this high rate of client satisfaction by turning client visions of business information goals into information systems reality, and by integrating the most current proven methodologies and technology tools into clients' solutions.

The company's success is also evident in the recognition it has received. *Inc.* magazine listed HDC as one of the nation's 500 fastest-growing companies four years in a row. The employees of HDC continually receive commendation and letters of appreciation from clients they support, and are truly the key backbone of the company's quality service. The company is active in community service organizations and is a member of the chambers of commerce of Fairfax and Reston, Virginia, and other areas throughout the country.

A RECOGNIZED SERVICE PROVIDER

HDC leads in Internet and network technologies, delivering and maintaining client World Wide Web sites that include live video, audio, and database integration. Coupled with high-speed networks that include fiber, asynchronous transfer mode (ATM), and simple network management protocol (SNMP), HDC provides the

best service and value in the area. As a company, HDC utilizes a process of the latest proven technologies, tools, and methodologies to provide outstanding quality in the design, development and testing, and integration of software applications into its clients' environment.

The design and development of the HDC Data Center include facilities management, customer help desk operations, computer center operations, and disaster recovery and backup, as well as an integrated national communication network.

HDC prides itself on providing total solutions to the health care industry that enable caregivers to concentrate on their patients instead of computer services. To that end, the company's Healthcare Systems Group offers a full suite of products and services designed for outpatient ambulatory care centers and clinical environments operating within federal and state governments, as well as private health care settings. These services enable health care providers to deliver quality care while efficiently managing their practices.

Additionally, HDC provides a full array of services in support of the prime business areas, including information technology (IT), project management, strategic planning, process reengineering, configuration management, modernization, office automation, data management, specialized programming, system integration, user support and LAN administration, documentation, education, training, and system maintenance.

Expertise on the World Wide Web, Internet and intranet, LAN/WAN/ADP communications, and cabling are among the most current and highly sought services also available to clients.

DEDICATED EMPLOYEES

HDC attracts and retains experienced and dedicated em-

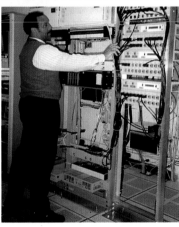

ployees by matching employees' talents to some of the most exciting and challenging opportunities in the industry. To attract and retain people with superior technical skills in an industry where the competition is fierce, HDC takes the hiring process a step further, making a serious effort to meet the needs of employees as well as the needs of clients.

HDC encourages the development of partnerships between its employees and clients, ultimately "matching" the two. In addition, employees are viewed as HDC ambassadors who represent both their employer and the organizations they serve.

Providing quality personnel resources to its distinct clientele is made possible by the maintenance of a constant and aggressive recruitment program. Because HDC encourages mobility and growth within the company, there is very little employee attrition. This creates a stable work environment in the midst of an ever changing industry.

Providing a good quality of life is also very important. HDC's location is conveniently close to Washington and allows its employees to take advantage of the cultural offerings of the nation's capital, while also giving them access to nearby Maryland and Virginia suburbs and some of the best school systems in the nation.

CLOCKWISE FROM TOP: THE COMPUTER CENTER—OPEN SEVEN DAYS A WEEK, 24 HOURS A DAY—SUPPLIES DEVELOPMENT, YEAR 2000 CONVERSION, AND DISASTER RECOVERY TO KEY GOVERNMENT AGENCIES.

HDC PROVIDES SIMPLE SOLUTIONS FOR THE HEALTH CARE INDUSTRY, INCLUDING AN ADVANCED COMPUTERIZED PATIENT RECORD AND COMPLETE PRACTICE MANAGEMENT SYSTEMS.

PAYING ATTENTION TO COST, QUALITY, INTEGRATION, AND SUPPORT, HDC PROVIDES COMMUNICATION AND INTERNET/INTRANET SERVICES TO FEDERAL AND COMMERCIAL CUSTOMERS.

A S THE WORLD'S LARGEST SUPPLIER OF SOFTWARE FOR INFORMATION management, and the world's second-largest software company, Oracle Corporation operates in more than 90 countries. The multibillion-dollar company employs nearly 30,000 people dedicated to providing customers worldwide with software solutions, consulting, education, and support. ◆ The company's products include

Oracle® Universal Server®, which is capable of managing virtually any type of multimedia information; a complete suite of developer tools; and application products for financial management, human resources, and manufacturing. Oracle backs up its software with Oracle Worldwide Support, a seven-day-a-week, 24-hour-a-day assistance program that ensures the company's products deliver maximum utility to customers.

KEEPING THE WORLD CONNECTED

Oracle software is the world's favorite solution for client/server computing and is leading the transformation to a networked society through the next wave of information processing, Network Computing. The software is compatible with almost every popular computer, from the smallest laptop to the very largest supercomputer,

and can be used to manage everything from personal information to giant corporations.

"Like petroleum a century ago, computer software has become the most important industry on earth," according to Lawrence J. Ellison, Oracle's chairman and chief executive officer. "Just as oil powered the modern industrial

age, software is the fuel of the information highway. It is not yet the world's biggest business, but it is the key to the operation of the information age."

Oracle not only produces the software that keeps the world in business, it provides consulting and support services to tailor its software to each customer's needs. Recently ranked as the fourth-largest client/server consulting organization in the world, Oracle Services helps customers realize rapid business benefits from information technologies.

A GOVERNMENT PRESENCE

Oracle Corporation was established in 1977 in Redwood Shores, California, and opened its Washington office—which houses Oracle Government—in 1983. Dedicated to serving all levels of government and education, Oracle Government is the foremost information management company for governments worldwide. For almost a decade, the vast majority of U.S. defense and civil agency programs have relied on Oracle for guidance in implementing new information solutions.

Coupling its heritage of technology innovation with an understanding of the customer's people, processes, and business problems, Oracle is viewed as a long-term strategic partner by many of its customers. To that end, Oracle Government opened an Advanced Technology Center (ATC) in Herndon, Virginia, to allow customers to see leading-edge information solutions in action before buying them. The ATC houses advanced enterprise computer hardware and software from

ORACLE'S VISION IS TO "CREATE THE NETWORKED SOCIETY," LINKING INDIVIDUALS, BUSINESSES, SCHOOLS, AND GOVERNMENTS WITH A COMMON GLOBAL INFRASTRUCTURE: NETWORK COMPUTING ARCHITECTURE.

Oracle and its business partners. The mission of the ATC is to help customers at all levels of the government visualize and experience new technologies in real-world environments.

"Through the ATC, we offer government customers a glimpse of the enterprise of the future," explains Jay Nussbaum, senior vice president and general manager of Oracle Government. "With technology advancing so rapidly, customers are faced with a dilemma: either risk investing in unproven systems or risk falling behind in productivity and effectiveness. The ATC was conceived to eliminate this dilemma."

Oracle sees information technology as the key to a government that works better and costs less. The ATC demonstrates ways to improve the government process—in operations, decision support, collaboration among users and agencies, and electronic commerce.

NETWORK COMPUTING— THE FUTURE IS NOW

The explosive growth of the Internet and intranets has provided a common global infrastructure to fuel a "networked society" that spans individuals, small businesses, governments, and multinational corporations. The maturing of this infrastructure signals a new phase of network computing that requires real business transactions, data-driven multimedia content, and interactive information access via self-service Web applications. Oracle, the Internet and network computing solutions company, is positioned to drive the next phase of ubiquitous service for individuals and corporations.

"All mature networks like TV and telephone have the same model—simple appliances with sophisticated and powerful networks," says Ellison. "Users shouldn't have to worry about the underlying technology. And corporate customers shouldn't

be left stranded with old technologies that don't work together."

Oracle recently introduced Network Computing Architecture™, a common set of technologies that will allow all PCs, network computers, and other devices to communicate with all Web servers, database servers, and application servers over any network. Network Computing Architecture allows mainframes, client/server, Internet and intranets, and distributed object software to work together, linking people and companies. In contrast with the PC-centric computing model that focuses on independent users and computation, Network Computing Architecture recognizes the increasing importance of "the network" to enhance communication and deliver a wide array of information on demand.

The idea for the Network Computer was conceived during a meeting with President Clinton and Vice President Gore. One day every school in America will be able to provide each student with a computer, making network computers as commonplace as telephones. Oracle's vision for the future is an age of computing that fully exploits the potential of high-speed networks while ensuring that end-user devices are priced low enough to accommodate everyone. With the phenomenal growth Oracle Corporation has experienced in recent years, Ellison has bright hopes for the company's future as well. "With continued good fortune, we could wind up the most successful firm in the software business," he says. "We're certainly going to try."

ORACLE GOVERNMENT IS A STRATEGIC PARTNER TO CUSTOMERS IN THE PUBLIC SECTOR THROUGHOUT THE UNITED STATES AND AROUND THE WORLD.

SHERIKON, INC.

SHERIKON, INC. IS A PROFESSIONAL SERVICES AND CUSTOM manufacturing company in its second decade of continued success. Since its modest beginnings in 1984 with only two employees, consistent customer satisfaction has made SHERIKON one of the fastest-growing companies in the country. ♦ Now a global firm with more than 1,000 employees, SHERIKON is large enough to deliver complex solutions, yet small enough

to give personal attention to every customer. Management and cost containment issues are universal, and SHERIKON's unique expertise easily accommodates the requirements of each individual client. The company offers creative, innovative, cost-effective solutions that are on time and within budget.

SHERIKON's broad range of disciplines brings solutions to the needs of the 21st century. Its employees have diverse backgrounds, including academic, government, military, and commercial sectors. SHERIKON offers expertise in all of the following disciplines: engineering, health care services, electronic repair and calibration, project management, information systems, integrated logistics,

health service logistics, decision analysis, cost/financial analysis, precision manufacturing, and specialized services.

Currently, 80 percent of SHERIKON's business comes from government contracts. "Our corporate headquarters is located here—in the Washington area—because this is where the decision makers and the money are," says Edward R. Fernandez, president and founder. Yet, in an attempt to diversify its client base, the company is striving for a 50-50 split between commercial and government clients, while maintaining half of its government focus on defense-oriented contracts.

Fernandez is committed to keeping his company on the leading edge of business technology

and scientific advancement. "To accomplish this," he explains, "SHERIKON has established the facilities and provided the resources necessary to support both our clients' and employees' needs for achievement across a broad front. Our record for expanding into new technological arenas and geographical regions attests to the success of our methods."

With the corporate headquarters in Chantilly, Virginia, SHERIKON has offices in Los Alamitos and San Diego, California; Virginia Beach, Crystal City, and Quantico, Virginia; San Antonio and Aransas Pass, Texas; Frederick, Maryland; New Orleans, Louisiana; and Harrisburg, Pennsylvania. In addition, the company also has four offices in Orlando, Florida, including a location at Kennedy Space Center.

THE SOURCE FOR EXCELLENCE

SHERIKON's reputation is built on more than being a business leader. Honesty and integrity are top priorities with Fernandez, who says, "From the day I founded SHERIKON in 1984, the company has achieved continuous growth and profitability. The basic belief with which I started has not altered over the years: Deliver value to your client, and respect and reward your staff. The application of these practices continues to ensure the highest possible level of satisfaction for our customers.

"SHERIKON's knowledgeable and professional staff will always work together with our clients to produce value-added results that enhance the reputation

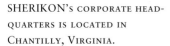

SHERIKON'S CORPORATE HEADQUARTERS IS LOCATED IN CHANTILLY, VIRGINIA.

of all concerned," adds Fernandez. ▶
"Our goal has been, and continues
to be, superior performance at a
reasonable cost."

Fernandez also notes, "As
our mission statement proclaims,
SHERIKON is committed to high
standards and the vigorous pursuit
of principled growth. We look
forward to the challenges ahead
and to maintaining our position
as the Source for Excellence."

PEOPLE POWER

M y assets go home every
night," Fernandez says,
referring to the people behind
his company. "The employees
are the assets of this company,"
explains Fernandez. "I'm very
proud of them."

And Fernandez goes to great
lengths to select employees who
share his standard of excellence,
high ethical standards, and team
spirit. He admits to having a pa-
ternalistic view of his company,
and the quality of life the company provides its employees is a
high priority.

Located 30 minutes outside
the nation's capital, Fernandez
sought a spot for his corporate
offices that provides employees
with "as many windows as possible" and beautifully landscaped
areas surrounding the offices. He
also sought space away from con-
gested highways so his employees
would not have to spend as much
time as many other commuters in
the Washington area getting to
and from work.

At SHERIKON, employees
are not only appreciated, they are
also recognized for their years of
service. Longevity awards—gold
logo pins—are presented quarterly
to employees who have worked
one, three, five, and 10 years with
the company.

RECOGNIZED LEADER

S HERIKON is recognized in
national publications, as well
as by industry peers, for the professional services and precision

products it provides to government, commercial, and international clients. SHERIKON was
on the Washington Technology
Fast 50 list in 1990, 1991, 1992,
and 1993. It was listed as one of
the 500 fastest-growing firms in
the nation in 1992 and 1993 by
Inc. magazine.

The company was on the
Hispanic Fastest Growing 500
list every year from 1992 through
1996. During those same five years,
it was recognized as one of the top
100 fastest-growing companies by
Hispanic Business magazine. In
addition, SHERIKON received the
Small Business Administration's
Award for Excellence in 1995. In
1995 and 1996, SHERIKON also
won the FastTrack Award—sponsored by Arthur Andersen, Riggs
Bank, and the *Washington Business
Journal*—for being one of the fastest-growing businesses in the

Washington metropolitan area.
SHERIKON and its subsidiaries
are extending their global reach.
By working with more customers
than ever before, the company is
expanding its capability and resources, which results in unprecedented value to customers and
even more robust relationships.
Process automation and business
management process engineering
lead the developmental thrust.

SHERIKON's Source for
Excellence is its people, who remain dedicated to providing the
company's customers superior
value and unequaled support.
Continued strengthening of its
professional workforce through
selective hiring, advanced education, and professional training
will continue to set SHERIKON
apart, and place it in the forefront for outstanding customer
satisfaction.

SHERIKON HAS A NATIONWIDE
NETWORK OF OFFICES, INCLUDING
ONE IN ORLANDO AT THE KENNEDY
SPACE CENTER (LEFT).

EDWARD R. FERNANDEZ, PRESIDENT
AND CEO OF SHERIKON, INC.
(RIGHT)

WHEN K. DAVID BOYER JR. AND FELICITY G. BELFORD founded TROY Systems, Inc. in 1984, they had a vision: to establish TROY as a world-class provider of leading-edge technologies, solutions, and value-added services that would revolutionize its customers' ability to access and manage vital information. Today, this vision is a reality. The Washington-based company has offices throughout the Middle Atlantic states and provides government and commercial clients around the world with information solutions designed to help them grow their businesses.

"Businesspeople around the world operating within government and private industry share a universal concern," explains Boyer, who serves as president and chief executive officer, "the twin challenges of managing change and maximizing the use of information and technology." TROY's mission is to assist its clients in strategically using information and technology as force multipliers to maximize their competitive posture in the global marketplace.

TROY is an award-winning information technology (IT) company that has built its success and client satisfaction by designing and safeguarding the technology requirements of its customers. Since its founding, TROY, a minority-owned business, has grown its technology base and personnel force to more than 350 professionals specializing in bringing the most secure IT-based solutions to its wide range of federal, Department of Defense, and commercial customers.

"We started out in the early 1980s helping people share information," adds Belford, executive vice president and chief operating officer. "We were at the front of the wave, and we're staying on the crest."

A HISTORY OF RAPID GROWTH

TROY focuses on growth in high-end technology services by leveraging its core businesses. TROY currently offers health information services, Internet/intranet technology, information systems security, information technology, and management services across market segments. TROY's technical support concentrates on infrastructure and modernization, improved communications, and integration of commercial off-the-shelf software. "We play a vital role in information management, safeguarding and maintaining the integrity of information," explains Don Celata, vice president of operations.

"Information security and health care systems are the fastest-growing areas at TROY," according to Bennett Gold, director of business development. "Troy currently manages some of the largest health information databases in the world, including the management of U.S. Army records." While the U.S. government currently represents roughly 90 percent of TROY's client base, the company is rapidly expanding its list of commercial clients through its subsidiary, the iNEX Corporation. iNEX is a leader in the rapidly growing area of Internet-based training (IBT), distance learning, and network-based services.

Experience has taught TROY to eliminate redundancies in technical and administrative systems. "We provide information technology products and services to clients in a cost-effective manner," adds Norm Walker, chief financial officer. "Working smart has made us highly competitive in the cost arena."

TROY SPECIALIZES IN HEALTH INFORMATION SERVICES, INTERNET/INTRANET TECHNOLOGY, INFORMATION SYSTEMS SECURITY, INFORMATION TECHNOLOGY, AND MANAGEMENT SERVICES.

PEOPLE POWER

A founding philosophy at TROY was to build a healthy work environment with an emphasis on professional growth and opportunity. TROY prides itself on being a highly competitive work environment where humor balances stress. With this commitment to opportunity comes responsibility, which Boyer does not take lightly.

"Just having a college degree is not good enough," Boyer says. "We all must be technologically sophisticated to be globally competitive." Boyer and Belford have developed an environment in which creativity is nurtured, innovation is rewarded, and initiative is appreciated. At TROY, there is an ongoing push for continuing education and training to meet the needs of the future. TROY's staff is committed to a lifetime of learning.

"Our company is a tool, a vehicle to accomplish educational and economic goals and address societal concerns," explains Boyer. "Jobs, education, and training are used to attract resources. We encourage the development of our employees."

Boyer and Belford also envision a diverse workforce in the future, and they're presenting their own company as a model. "We go the extra mile to ensure a composition reflective of the world at large in age, culture, and other areas," Boyer proudly states. "We're committed to minority development. Our workers are trained to excel. We do a lot of mentoring, and we practice what we preach. There's no glass ceiling here."

A RECOGNIZED LEADER AND INNOVATOR

Boyer and Belford's innovative approach has not gone unrecognized. In fact, during its brief existence, the company has been the recipient of a long list of honors. In 1991, Boyer received recognition from the Small Business

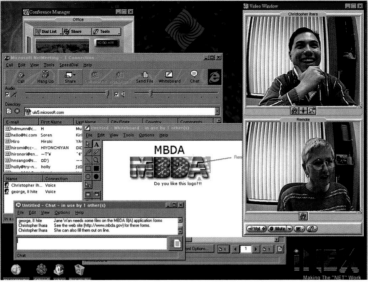

iNEX, A SUBSIDIARY OF TROY, PROVIDES STATE-OF-THE-ART INTERACTIVE MULTIMEDIA CONSULTING WITH SPECIALIZATION IN INTERNET-BASED DISTANCE LEARNING.

TROY'S VISION FOCUSES ON THE PROVISION OF TECHNOLOGIES, SOLUTIONS, AND SERVICES EMPOWERING CLIENTS TO ACCESS AND MANAGE VITAL INFORMATION.

Administration (SBA) by earning two awards on behalf of his company: the Minority Business Person of the Year and the Minority Small Business of the Year in the Washington Region. That same year, the U.S. Department of Commerce named Boyer the Regional Businessman of the Year, and the Minority Business Development Agency awarded TROY the Minority Small Business of the Year in the Washington Region.

In 1992, TROY received recognition from the SBA as the Small Business of the Year in the National Capital Region. The Clinton administration's 1993 National Performance Review program, under the direction of Vice President Al Gore, invited Boyer to share his insight into the government infrastructure by participating in a task force consisting of 10 prominent business leaders from across the nation. The resulting plans of the task force were used to promote the achievement of total quality management in government.

In 1994, TROY was recognized as one of the nation's 500 fastest-growing companies by *Inc.* magazine. Ernst & Young presented Boyer with the prestigious 1994 Greater Washington High Tech Entrepreneur of the Year

award. A year later, the company was designated a National Technology Fast 500 company by Technews, Inc. and Deloitte & Touche LLP. In 1996, the Northern Virginia Technology Council recognized TROY with its Fast 50 award. And in 1997, TROY received the prestigious Administrator's Award for Excellence from the U.S. Small Business Administration.

These accolades are evidence that Boyer and Belford's founding vision has indeed been realized. TROY Systems is an integral part of its clients' successes, and the principals intend to see that it remains so for many years to come.

ELLON PROVIDES A FULL RANGE OF BANKING AND INVESTMENT products and services to individuals, businesses, and institutions in the Washington, D.C., area. ◆ Mellon's diverse resources make it uniquely qualified to meet sophisticated investment and banking needs. Its 1993 acquisition of the Boston Company and 1994 merger with the Dreyfus Corporation, then the nation's

sixth-largest mutual fund company, positioned Mellon as the largest bank manager of mutual funds and among the largest investment management firms in the United States. Mellon's innovative use of technology and convenient delivery channels makes it a leader in serving the financial services needs of consumers and businesses.

For customers conducting their banking in person, Mellon Financial Centers combine the latest in banking technology with extended hours of operation and personalized service for one-stop shopping and unrivaled convenience, service, information, and choices. In addition to video banking and PC banking services, each Mellon Financial Center also features dedicated private banking professionals to provide affluent individuals and professional practices with

a single point of contact for Mellon's banking, asset management, investment, and jumbo mortgage services. For customers who prefer the convenience of banking by telephone or personal computer, Mellon provides a full selection of services 24 hours a day, seven days a week.

Mellon's broad array of services designed to meet the investment needs of local corporations includes a complete selection of paper-based and electronic cash management products to help manage cash flow. Its industry-leading master trust and global custody businesses offer securities processing, record keeping, safekeeping, securities lending, and foreign exchange services to institutional markets. Mellon also provides high-quality investment products and services to pension plans,

foundations, and endowments, as well as other tax-exempt organizations. Mellon's banking services for corporations and institutions include corporate banking, capital markets, middle market banking, lease financing, insurance premium financing, and asset-based lending for corporations and institutions.

With a diverse line of banking and investment products and services, Mellon is a financial services company with a bank at its core. As the financial services industry continues to evolve, Mellon is well positioned to meet the sophisticated financial services needs of its customers in the Washington area.

TO SOLIDIFY RELATIONSHIPS, INCREASE EMPLOYEE RESPONSIVENESS, AND EXPAND VALUE TO CLIENTS, MELLON FOSTERS TEAMWORK AND COOPERATION AMONG THE DIVERSE AREAS OF ITS ORGANIZATION. TEAMWORK PROMOTES INTERDEPENDENT CROSS-SELLING EFFORTS AMONG BUSINESS LINES.

T HE WHOLE POINT IN LAUNCHING SYLVEST," SAYS GARY S. Murray, chief executive officer and president, "was to create a company that could make a significant contribution to the computing industry— one with a single mission: to deliver successful, open systems solutions that work." In less than a decade, Sylvest Management Systems Corporation has built a reputation for doing just that. ♦ Today, one of the top

minority-owned companies in the country is a "soup to nuts" project problem solver. With nearly 200 employees, Sylvest is also one of the nation's fastest-growing companies. "We can attribute our growth to a number of factors," says William S. Strang, executive vice president. "But the biggest reason is the quality of work . . . which is why nearly all of our clients ask us back for more."

Revenue has increased 500 percent in the past four years, and the company continues to attract the best and brightest people in the industry to meet its growing demand for employees.

CORPORATE STRUCTURE

Sylvest, which was founded in 1987 by Murray and Strang, established its niche by integrating UNIX-based hardware and software. Its customer list includes a broad spectrum of federal, state, and local agencies, as well as prime contractors and a growing number of commercial entities.

The Federal Division forms strategic vendor relationships with leading hardware and software manufacturers. It also markets and distributes the company's General Services Administration schedule, in addition to meeting the information systems needs of federal customers. The division is also the company's program management and integration arm for long-term opportunities.

The Commercial Division customizes solutions for a broad range of large and medium-sized private-sector companies interested in areas such as enterprise network

management, enterprise reengineering, work group computing, customer management solutions, and Internet/intranet.

Sylvest's strength is in its consulting services, but the company also provides all the products and services customers require for total systems integration. While headquartered in a suburb of the nation's capital, Sylvest has branch offices in major cities across the country.

INDUSTRY LEADER

As a testament to its success, Sylvest has been recognized three times by *Washington Technology* magazine as one of the most rapidly growing high-technology companies in the Washington area. It has also been acknowledged by other national trade and business publications for outstanding growth and performance.

Inc. magazine has named Sylvest one of the top 500 privately held companies in the nation, and

Black Enterprise magazine has repeatedly named it one of the top 100 minority-owned businesses. The company has also been repeatedly noted as a Partner for Quality Contracting by the U.S. Department of Commerce for its work with the National Oceanic and Atmospheric Administration (NOAA).

Sylvest credits its employees as the company's most important asset. "Sylvest conducts its business with uncompromising integrity," says Murray. "We foster an environment in which high performance, teamwork, risk taking, innovation, and continuous improvement are encouraged and rewarded."

The company provides a creative environment where employees are encouraged to share their thoughts and ideas, and achievements are rewarded. Sylvest's astonishing growth and impeccable reputation within the industry attest to the success of this policy.

"SYLVEST CONDUCTS ITS BUSINESS WITH UNCOMPROMISING INTEGRITY," SAYS GARY S. MURRAY, PRESIDENT AND CEO OF SYLVEST (RIGHT). "WE FOSTER AN ENVIRONMENT IN WHICH HIGH PERFORMANCE, TEAMWORK, RISK TAKING, INNOVATION, AND CONTINUOUS IMPROVEMENT ARE ENCOURAGED AND REWARDED."

"WE CAN ATTRIBUTE OUR GROWTH TO A NUMBER OF FACTORS," SAYS WILLIAM S. STRANG, EXECUTIVE VICE PRESIDENT (LEFT). "BUT THE BIGGEST REASON IS THE QUALITY OF WORK . . . WHICH IS WHY NEARLY ALL OF OUR CLIENTS ASK US BACK FOR MORE."

SYTEL, INC.

DURING THE PAST DECADE, SYTEL, INC.—A LEADING INFORMATION technology consulting firm—has built a reputation for high-quality performance. Sytel strives to become a leader in the industry by capitalizing on its robust corporate infrastructure, superb managers and employees, and clear vision for the company's future. ♦ Founder, President, and Chief Executive Officer Jeannette Lee says Sytel focuses

on its information technology (IT) niche. Areas of expertise include LAN/WAN (local-area network/wide-area network), client/server and software engineering, imaging/work flow, and systems integration. In addition, the firm specializes in outsourcing, information systems security (INFOSEC), and engineering services. Lee says, "The goal is to become one of the leading information technology companies in the industry by applying cutting-edge technologies through a team of highly motivated, top quality technical talent."

Founded in 1987, Sytel has experienced average annual revenue growth of more than 100 percent to reach $30 million in 1996—a figure that is projected to double in 1997. Sytel strives for complete customer satisfaction.

Sytel's strong commitment to quality services has helped the Bethesda, Maryland, firm become one of the fastest-growing companies in the nation. In 1996, *Inc.* magazine listed Sytel as 37th on its list of the 500 Fastest Growing Private Companies in America and

the *Washington Business Journal* ranked it as eighth on its list of the Top 15 Largest Networking/Systems Companies in the Washington area. In 1995, the firm was ranked fifth in *Washington Technology*'s Fast 50.

THE COMPANY

From the start, Lee has had experience in managing chaos. During the year she started the company, Lee also got married, had a baby, and bought her first house. Today, she says the key is to manage an ideal mix of order and chaos. For a fast-growing company like Sytel, Lee's formula is 60 percent process and order, and 40 percent chaos. She says the latter promotes speed while inspiring creativity and imagination. Lee says Sytel employees know how to maximize (and capitalize on) many of the positive aspects of chaos, while overcoming some of the typical pitfalls associated with organizational chaos.

For major IT programs, Lee says Sytel is often the chosen teaming partner because it has

a proven track record as a major contributor to the success of team bids and has an excellent post-award performance record.

Sytel's program support is backed by a robust corporate infrastructure. There are five separate divisions to provide tailored solutions to a wide range of government organizations and commercial clients nationwide. The Network Engineering Division focuses on LAN and WAN connectivity. The Information Technology Division provides services for business process reengineering, rapid prototyping, database development, object-oriented design and programming, client/server applications, and open systems migration and right sizing.

Sytel's Outsourcing Services Division performs data center support activities, including operations, systems and applications programming, telecommunications, end-user training, and help desk and end-user support. The Aerospace Technology Division handles engineering support services, instrumentation engineering, communications and data systems, mechanical engineering systems, mission planning, and qualification and testing.

The Systems Integration Division provides products and integrated solutions, such as electronic imaging, document management, work flow automation, electronic commerce/electronic data interchange (EC/EDI), Internet and intranets, computer telephony, video teleconferencing, and multimedia. The division has successful relationships with leading PC and networking firms, including Panasonic, Dell, Compaq, Microsoft,

SYTEL WANTS TO BE RECOGNIZED FOR THE TALENT BEHIND THE NAME.

Hewlett Packard, Cisco, Cabletron, Oracle, and Sun.

All divisions report directly to the company's Executive Management Team, as do the managers of the Finance and Administration, Contracts, Sales and Marketing, Bids and Proposals, and Recruiting departments.

OUTSTANDING STAFF

Sytel is proud of its success in attracting high-quality managers and employees in a very competitive industry. It's part of Lee's vision for her company: "to build a highly professional corporate culture that fosters innovation, creativity, and maximum efficiency." It's a culture that "emphasizes corporate loyalty by giving fair and deserving short-term and long-term rewards to those who contribute to the future of Sytel."

Lee says the firm attracts and retains talented people by providing a challenging, yet nurturing, work environment. An emphasis on lifelong learning is one of the company's most attractive benefits, and the need to train and retrain employees is backed up with a tuition reimbursement plan and other innovative training initiatives. While Sytel uses recruiting methods that range from Internet postings to working with outplacement offices of large companies that are downsizing, manager and employee referrals are cred-

ited with attracting the most successful hires.

Sytel's managers are encouraged to be sensitive to the career path of each employee, and each person is given more responsibility and authority as the company grows. In a constant effort to reward innovation, business growth, and profitability, there are significant rewards and other incentives available for those who make exceptional contributions to the company.

THE FUTURE

Sytel's list of customers is ever expanding, and its officers and managers are convinced that— through ensuring quality control, concentrating on areas of expertise, providing solutions for customers, and expanding into the commercial market—the company always will continue to grow. However, Lee does not want growth for the sake of growth. She says quality always will be emphasized, and there will be rapid growth as long as it is well managed.

Sytel will continue to be a role model in the computer systems and telecommunications industry. Lee says the way to make this happen is to help Sytel's customers succeed. Her goal for Sytel is twofold: She wants her company to be an industry leader in the way it helps clients apply technologies to needs, which enables her customers to do more with less, yet she also wants Sytel

to be recognized for the talent behind the name. Sytel strives to become a model for attracting and retaining the best people in the industry, as well as for cultivating the talents of its staff.

According to Lee, the time is ripe for many companies to succeed. "Sytel is evolving constantly and has many big but very realizable dreams, and a clear vision of the future," she stresses. Confident that with Sytel, its partners, its people, and its clients all working together, Lee says, "We will succeed together."

SYTEL ATTRACTS AND RETAINS TALENTED PEOPLE BY PROVIDING A CHALLENGING, YET NURTURING, WORK ENVIRONMENT. THE EMPHASIS ON LIFELONG LEARNING IS ONE OF THE COMPANY'S MOST ATTRACTIVE BENEFITS (LEFT).

A STRONG COMMITMENT TO QUALITY SERVICES HAS HELPED SYTEL BECOME ONE OF THE FASTEST-GROWING COMPANIES IN THE NATION (RIGHT).

RELIABLE INTEGRATION SERVICES, INC. (RIS) IS A WOMAN-OWNED network systems integrator that has served a growing list of clients in the Washington area since its inception in 1988. Over the past decade, RIS has established its reputation as a technical expert, using state-of-the-art technology and remaining on the cutting edge of emerging telecommunication standards, such as asynchronous transfer mode (ATM). RIS is recognized as a leader in finding workable, affordable solutions to network integration and management problems. The company provides government and commercial clients with comprehensive network, telecommunications, and systems integration expertise, specializing in turnkey products and services for single and multiple vendor systems that require voice, data, video, and imaging transmission.

RIS also provides comprehensive network maintenance and support services, and has been revitalizing legacy technology computer network systems since its inception.

VALERIE PERLOWITZ (TOP RIGHT) WAS ONLY 26 YEARS OLD WHEN SHE FOUNDED RIS. SINCE IT BEGAN IN 1988, RIS HAS BECOME ONE OF THE MOST SUCCESSFUL NETWORK SYSTEMS INTEGRATORS IN THE MID-ATLANTIC REGION, AND PERLOWITZ HAS BECOME A PIONEER IN HER FIELD.

ARTHUR W. PIERSON

A FULL RANGE OF SERVICES

Valerie Perlowitz was only 26 years old when she founded RIS. "We were working on a Federal Aviation Administration subcontract for a former employer when they and the prime contractor, IBM, had a parting of the ways," explains Perlowitz, who also serves as RIS's president. "IBM asked us if we wanted to start our own company and take over the subcontract. We had next to nothing in start-up capital, but we accepted the proposal."

Since that fateful decision in 1988, RIS has become one of the most successful network systems integrators in the mid-Atlantic region, and Perlowitz has become a pioneer in her field by developing a comprehensive metrics-based methodology for network integration.

The staff at RIS has extensive experience in the analysis, planning, design, implementation, and maintenance of large information and communications systems. Keenly focused on solving difficult interoperability issues, RIS provides a full range of affordable solutions that meet diverse networking requirements. Services offered by RIS include consulting and feasibility study, network design and installation, engineering, standards selection, software development support, education and training, program management, systems and facilities management, operations services, and preventive maintenance.

AN OUTSTANDING LEADER

Today, Perlowitz is widely recognized as a technology leader in the Greater Washington area. She was the first of only two women to receive a Commonwealth of Virginia appointment to the board of directors of the Virginia Technology Council. In 1996, she was listed among the Top 100 Women in Computing by *Open Computing*. In 1994, she also founded the nonprofit Women in Technology in response to a growing regional demand to foster professional development and business networking opportunities for women at all levels in technology fields.

Largely as a result of Perlowitz's leadership, her company continues its rapid growth. But she always shares the credit with her staff, saying she only hires the best. As for the future, Perlowitz has nothing but a bright forecast for RIS. She cheerfully predicts, "We'll measure our success by that of our clients, and the practical application of technology has shown us that there is no limit to what can be achieved."

ARTHUR W. PIERSON

ARTHUR W. PIERSON

SpaceWorks, Inc. is one of the fastest-growing privately held companies in the Washington area. It has found its niche by creating software products that help business customers conduct electronic commerce over the Internet. The firm, which was incorporated in 1993, is the leading provider of complete electronic commerce software solutions and counts Fortune 500 companies among its clientele.

SpaceWorks develops, markets, and supports a suite of business-oriented electronic commerce software applications that can be used on the Internet and through corporate computer networks or "intranets." Its customers use these interactive products to automate critical business-to-business activities related to supply chain management, order processing, and fulfillment.

Complete Solutions

SpaceWorks' World Wide Web-based software applications can be implemented as is, or customized to meet any customer's specific business needs. The products consist of a library of functional, reusable objects and HTML or Java-based user interface templates, which enable the delivery of complete solutions or add-on features to new clients in shorter turnaround times than if the client used development tools to build their own applications in-house.

The turnkey solutions in the SpaceWorks product suite can be linked to one or more back-office legacy systems. This allows a corporation's trading partners to gain real-time, electronic access to information stored in numerous disparate data repositories through a single graphical interface. Since the products are Internet based, they enable businesses to use a single public and private intranet system to connect with both their internal corporate users and their external business trading partners.

The Company's Niche

SpaceWorks is helping companies reduce their operating costs in managing transactions from suppliers, channel partners, and business clients by moving away from traditional telephone- and paper-based tasks. "Today, our software solutions enable buyers to communicate directly with

JOHN HARRINGTON

the back-office system that fills the order, tracks the order, and stores product inventory and price information in the catalog for creating the order," says David MacSwain, president and chief executive officer. Envisioning global 24x7 office environments in the near future, MacSwain says that ordering from paper catalogs through a person at a central order desk is already obsolete.

"The Internet phenomenon has laid down the railroad tracks for electronic commerce to happen between any two partners, from anywhere, at any time," says MacSwain. "Even now we're seeing the creation of 'virtual warehouses' in the marketplace as all the supply chain partners migrate to doing business electronically."

The Future

In a rapidly changing marketplace, SpaceWorks is well positioned in the dynamic environment created by the customers it

JOHN HARRINGTON

serves. Although the firm is small and young, it is attracting the interest of larger, more established companies that see the value in implementing SpaceWorks' turnkey software solutions.

Meanwhile, company officials project a bright future with their commercial clients. Says MacSwain, "I think this marketplace is going to explode."

CLOCKWISE FROM TOP LEFT: SpaceWorks' Internet-based electronic commerce software applications help companies boost revenues while slashing the cost of doing business.

SpaceWorks President and CEO David MacSwain sees dramatic growth in the company's future.

SpaceWorks' software completely automates mission critical order processing activities by creating a self-service environment.

Business is booming at Unitel Corporation, a full-service telemarketing firm that is reaping the benefits of the current business trends of downsizing and outsourcing. ♦ Founded in 1991 by Douglas Palley and S. Tien Wong with a $250,000 investment, Unitel has grown into one of the strongest telemarketing firms in the country. In addition to its headquarters in McLean, Virginia, there are call centers in McLean and in Frostburg, Maryland, with plans for a third call center to open in 1997.

THE COMPANY

Unitel is an award-winning, full-service, integrated marketing company that specializes in providing outsourced teleservices solutions. The company develops and delivers customized business-to-business and business-to-consumer sales, marketing, and customer care solutions for a wide range of corporate clients.

Today, the company has more than 400 workstations with computers and advanced telephone equipment for a staff to receive as many as 150,000 calls each day, or more than 1 million per week. It is a real contrast with the early days when seven employees crowded around a long, wooden table in a one-room office in Arlington, Virginia. Now the company operates 24 hours a day, 365

THE FASTEST-GROWING TELESERVICES FIRM IN THE NATION IS ALSO THE MOST HIGHLY DECORATED. UNITEL HAS BEEN RECOGNIZED ON NUMEROUS OCCASIONS BY *Inc.*, *Telemarketing*, AND *TeleProfessional* MAGAZINES (TOP).

IN KEEPING WITH A CORPORATE PHILOSOPHY OF CONTINUOUS IMPROVEMENT, UNITEL CONSTANTLY SEARCHES FOR NEW AND MORE EFFECTIVE METHODS TO SERVE CLIENTS AND ADD VALUE TO THEIR CUSTOMER RELATIONSHIPS (BOTTOM).

MICHAEL CARPENTER PHOTOGRAPHY

MICHAEL CARPENTER PHOTOGRAPHY

days a year. Many clients require round-the-clock service with live operators, but Unitel also provides customized voice messaging for many clients during their off hours.

In an increasingly global economy, Unitel also provides teleservices representatives (TSRs) who are fluent in one or more foreign languages, including Spanish, French, German, Korean, Japanese, Vietnamese, Cantonese, and Mandarin. Due to the diverse population in the Washington area, the company has access to a large pool of bilingual job applicants.

In planning for the future, Unitel has retained Ernst & Young's accounting services in preparation for a public stock offering in the near future. "We want to grow," explains Palley, "but we also want to maintain our reputation as being the finest service bureau in the country."

EXCELLENT EMPLOYEES

Unitel takes pride in its home-grown staff. "Many people start out on the phones, and then are promoted within the company," says Palley. "When we fill new positions, we look internally first."

Palley describes the work environment as fun, but demanding. He says the staff is well trained to handle the state-of-the-art tools at their disposal. The TSRs are instructed to start anew with each call and treat each caller as special.

Unitel's conscientious, multi-step recruitment process is aimed at assuring only high-quality, professional, articulate employees are hired. All TSRs are screened via telephone for college background, work experience, intelligence, articulation, communication, clarity, pitch, intonation, and enthusiasm. Potential employees fill out a comprehensive application. A Unitel-developed automated skills test is administered to certify that applicants meet the company's high standards.

Trained interviewers evaluate sales/marketing and customer service skills; reading, spelling, and data entry abilities; and personality, appearance, self-motivation, and other qualities. References are checked to confirm interviewers' findings and verify the accuracy of information on applications.

Experience, education, voice, computer, and interactive skills are among the most significant qualities Unitel seeks in TSRs. The company estimates the typical Unitel representative is nearly 35 years old, and has eight to 10 years of business experience, usually in sales, marketing, and/or customer service. Nearly 100 percent of Unitel's telephone representatives have some college experience, and more than 70 percent have four-year college degrees.

QUALITY ASSURANCE

Unitel's Quality First system encompasses every employee and is tailored to each client's special requirements. Quality assurance is the function of managers, supervisors, and dedicated quality assurance managers.

In keeping with a corporate philosophy of continuous improvement, Unitel constantly searches for new and more effective methods to serve clients and add value to their customer relationships. In pursuit of this goal, accountability is crucial. Client service managers monitor all computer-generated project reports and prepare project status reports and summaries that are analyzed by top management.

Customers' perceptions are gauged on a real-time basis through call monitoring and instant feedback from TSRs. Call resolution statistics for individual TSRs and overall shift statistics reveal on a daily basis how well Unitel is interacting with customers. Client

feedback also helps determine customers' perceptions.

Client service managers' daily contact with clients often yields valuable feedback. Clients receive daily and weekly reports and may monitor TSRs. Clients are also encouraged to share their findings with Unitel's managers.

RECOGNITION

The fastest-growing teleservices firm in the nation is also the most highly decorated. Unitel is the only consecutive-year winner of the industry's most prestigious award: the 1994, 1995, and 1996 MVP Quality Award from *Telemarketing* magazine. In addition, Unitel won the 1995 and 1996 Award for Call Center Excellence (ACCE) from *TeleProfessional* magazine.

The MVP and ACCE awards are bestowed upon organizations that embody total commitment to client service and quality performance. Unitel is now ranked as the 35th-largest call center in the country as rated by *Telemarketing*

magazine in 1996, and in July 1996, the magazine named Unitel the fastest-growing telemarketing firm in the country. The company is also ranked as one of the 50 fastest-growing private companies in the nation in *Inc.* magazine's 1997 Inc. 500. The awards reflect Unitel's capacity to expand while maintaining the highest quality, a trait that will ensure its success for many years to come.

▶ MICHAEL CARPENTER PHOTOGRAPHY

UNITEL'S QUALITY FIRST SYSTEM ENCOMPASSES EVERY EMPLOYEE AND IS TAILORED TO EACH CLIENT'S SPECIAL REQUIREMENTS. QUALITY ASSURANCE IS THE FUNCTION OF MANAGERS, SUPERVISORS, AND DEDICATED QUALITY ASSURANCE MANAGERS (TOP).

IN ADDITION TO ITS HEADQUARTERS IN MCLEAN, VIRGINIA, THERE ARE CALL CENTERS IN MCLEAN AND IN FROSTBURG, MARYLAND, WITH PLANS FOR A THIRD CALL CENTER TO OPEN IN 1997 (BOTTOM).

▶ MICHAEL CARPENTER PHOTOGRAPHY

W HEN MAINFRAMES AND MINICOMPUTERS DOMINATED THE computing environment, protecting information was relatively easy. Today, however, those large machines have given way to distributed environments: efficient, flexible, and wide open to information theft. AXENT is committed to securing organizations' information resources with products and services that answer this growing business challenge. AXENT's commitment has enabled the company to secure a position as the leading information security solution provider in the industry throughout 1996.

With branch offices across the country and distribution and sales offices around the world, AXENT's security technology is used by Fortune 1000 companies and governments worldwide to effectively secure and protect information systems in heterogeneous computing environments.

INDUSTRY LEADER

A XENT successfully executed an initial public offering in April 1996, following its 1995 spin-off of Raxco, Inc. Emphasizing information security management, the company is growing approximately 50 percent a year.

At a time when most companies fear computer break-ins, AXENT helps companies determine how to protect their data from intruders by automating the implementation of information security policies tailored to individual businesses. AXENT's software products control access to data in computer systems and monitor systems for suspicious events and nonconformances with established security policies. Such technology also assists businesses in addressing consumer concerns about losing privacy during an era when a wide variety of personal information is just a keystroke away.

Additionally, as more people work from remote sites, AXENT provides technologies to authenticate users.

PRODUCT SOLUTION

A XENT views information security as more than just a technology issue. It is a critical business issue. AXENT's Omni-Guard suite of software products enables organizations to centrally manage information security across multiple computing platforms. It also allows the user to define security policies as well as manage and enforce them. Security procedures and guidelines are established without regard to the computing platform, taking diverse systems and creating a cohesive whole that can be evaluated according to a single set of security policy rules. Omni-Guard also provides enhanced data confidentiality, access control, user administration, and intrusion detection.

SERVICES

T o complement its software offerings, AXENT provides consulting services for organizations that may require a particular combination of education, training, strategic consulting, and technology. Available in prepackaged as well as custom modules, services include training, implementation, security analysis, policy development, and disaster-recovery planning.

AXENT has positioned itself as one of the 21st century's key partners, with a mission to protect the organization's sensitive information from intrusion, theft, and misuse.

AXENT'S OMNIGUARD SUITE OF SOFTWARE PRODUCTS ENABLES ORGANIZATIONS TO CENTRALLY MANAGE INFORMATION SECURITY ACROSS MULTIPLE COMPUTING PLATFORMS.

ARTHUR J. MORRIS ESTABLISHED THE MORRIS PLAN INSURANCE Society in 1917 as the first credit life insurance company in the United States. It guaranteed consumer loans for thousands of working-class people who had borrowed money for necessary goods and services. Known today as ReliaStar Employer Financial Services Company, the firm serves as the worksite marketing

division of ReliaStar Bankers Security Life Insurance Company, specializing in payroll deducted life insurance products.

ReliaStar Employer Financial Services Company President Jim Cochran says the tradition Morris started nearly a century ago continues today. "In Morris' own words, 'No man's debt should outlive him.' This is a concept he proved by offering the first credit life insurance policy in 1917," explains Cochran. "Today, our worksite marketing coverages protect the needs of the masses, not just the elite. We provide coverage for working men and women and their families through the most convenient and logical channel— the workplace."

The Past

By 1967, Bankers Security Life was licensed to do business in all 50 states and the District of Columbia, and in 1977, the company wrote its first large payroll deduction case for Grumman Aircraft Corporation of Long Island. It was the beginning of a profitable tradition for the company. By the early 1980s, the company was recognized by large retail insurance firms as having one of the best payroll deduction programs available.

In 1995, ReliaStar Financial Corp. acquired Bankers Security Life. The Bankers name changed, but the company continues its tradition of serving the payroll deduction market with universal life, whole life, and term insurance products.

The acquisition by ReliaStar now gives ReliaStar Employer

Financial Services Company an affiliation with a strong and diversified financial services organization. Currently, ReliaStar is the 12th-largest publicly held life insurance company in the United States. Headquartered in Minneapolis and founded in 1885, ReliaStar is a holding company whose subsidiaries provide financial security to individuals and businesses through individual life insurance and annuities, employee benefits, retirement plans, life and health reinsurance, mutual funds, and personal finance education programs. The company's goal is to be a lifetime partner delivering integrated financial solutions to its customers.

The Future

ReliaStar Employer Financial Services Company sees quality service as the way to succeed in worksite marketing. To achieve that goal, the company stands ready with advanced technology to adapt to changes in today's workplace. Employees and clients are regularly surveyed to detect where change is needed. The latest technology is being used in an attempt to provide service as simply as possible.

ReliaStar Employer Financial Services Company uses a paperless enrollment system. Potential policyholders simply have to sign via a laptop computer to enroll in the insurance program, thereby avoiding the cumbersome paperwork traditionally associated with insurance policies. In addition, the policies are fully portable, which means employees can retain their

coverage even if they leave the employer who originally provided access to the insurance program.

"We found not only a niche, but ways to maintain our leading-edge role," says Cochran. "We think this market will grow, since two-thirds of the people who work do not have an insurance agent of their own. These people represent the vast population who can benefit from better access to insurance protection. We are there for the masses, not only for life, but for all benefit needs through employers."

A PAPERLESS ENROLLMENT SYSTEM ALLOWS POTENTIAL POLICYHOLDERS TO SIGN VIA A LAPTOP COMPUTER (TOP).

RELIASTAR EMPLOYER FINANCIAL SERVICES COMPANY IS LOCATED IN ARLINGTON, VIRGINIA (BOTTOM).

COMBINING THE VERY LATEST TECHNOLOGY, OUTSTANDING SERVICE, and technical expertise, Nortel Communications Systems (NCS) keeps its business customers one step ahead in the rapidly changing communications world. ♦ NCS—consisting of Nortel Communications Systems, Inc. and its affiliated companies, Bell Atlantic Meridian Systems and TTS Meridian Systems, Inc.—has operations throughout the eastern states from Virginia to Maine, as well as in California, other western states, and across Canada. NCS is Northern Telecom's (Nortel's) largest authorized U.S. distributor of the Meridian 1, a telecommunications system for large businesses and organizations. The company also sells and services the Nortel Norstar system for smaller call volumes, the Nortel COMPANION wireless communications system, and a wide array of customized applications for voice mail, call center management, computer-telephony integration (CTI), and many other communications and networking solutions.

ENGINEERS INSTALL NORTEL COMPANION, AN ADVANCED, IN-BUILDING, PORTABLE TELEPHONE SYSTEM FOR BUSINESS (TOP).

NCS IS A SINGLE SOURCE FOR THE PRODUCTS, PEOPLE, AND KNOWLEDGE NEEDED TO SEAMLESSLY INTEGRATE MULTIPLE TECHNOLOGIES INTO ONE FOCUSED APPROACH TO BUSINESS COMMUNICATIONS CHALLENGES (BOTTOM).

INDUSTRY LEADERS

In the Washington area, NCS operates through Bell Atlantic Meridian Systems, a joint-venture partnership between Bell Atlantic and Nortel, two powerful industry leaders.

Nortel, a 100-year-old company, offers one of the broadest choices of products for designing, building, and integrating digital networks—for information, entertainment, education, and business—around the globe.

Drawing on the power of Nortel, NCS is well positioned in a world where businesses are no longer bound by geographic lines or regional loyalties. The company offers far-reaching value as a single source for the products, people, and knowledge needed to seamlessly integrate multiple technologies into one focused approach to business communications challenges.

Behind every product NCS sells and services is Nortel's Evergreen commitment, which takes the pressure off deciding when to update a system with new features and functionality. Nortel products offer clear migration paths that let customers update software effectively, conveniently, and quickly. In addition, Nortel's adherence to such standards as the telephony application programming interface (TAPI) and telephony services application interface (TSAPI) provides a common means for communications applications to control telephony functions for data, fax, and voice calls.

RELIABLE PRODUCTS

Meridian 1 and Norstar are among the most reliable, advanced, and easy-to-use business telecommunications systems. The largest of the Meridian family, the Meridian SL-100, has the power to run intelligent multimedia networks of up to 60,000 digital lines. On the smaller side, the Norstar-PLUS Modular ICS system enables companies to affordably integrate voice, video, data, and wireless technologies.

Nortel COMPANION, an advanced, in-building, portable telephone system for business, is fully adaptable to both the Meridian 1 and Norstar systems. As users walk and talk on the COMPANION, their conversation is picked up by a base station—and as they move, it hands the call to another base station.

COMPUTER-TELEPHONY INTEGRATION

In the area of CTI, customer demand is growing rapidly. To address the need, NCS has established regional High Impact Technology (HIT) teams consisting of specialized application engineers and system integrators, who are

trained and experienced in delivering and installing advanced applications. The teams work within the sales office and provide pre-sales support and project integration. NCS also has established a design center called the Advanced Technologies Group (ATG), where creativity and new design approaches are actively encouraged in the full integration of voice and computing systems. In ATG's fully outfitted laboratory, customers can see that NCS is clearly more than a provider of standard telephone systems.

OUTSTANDING SERVICE

NCS backs its technology and expertise with a strong commitment to service. Each system NCS sells and installs comes with a parts-and-labor warranty for one year after installation. It also comes with the dedication of the NCS account support team, which regularly evaluates the customer's system to make sure it meets changing business objectives.

Strategically located Customer Support Centers (CSCs) provide service 24 hours a day, 365 days a year. Remote diagnostic computers monitor systems and identify potential problems before they affect daily operations. Should an emergency arise, telecommunications professionals are ready to respond. Through remote diagnostic capabilities, a large percentage of service calls can be solved over the phone.

With the NCS 2-Hour Service Guarantee, the company guarantees that, in an emergency, NCS will fix the problem remotely, or be on-site working on the problem within two hours. If the deadline is not met, the customer receives one month's free maintenance.

CUSTOMER SATISFACTION

To gauge its performance, NCS regularly conducts a measurement of customer satisfaction—and each year the index has grown. The steady increase is due to a customer-first attitude, which has been ingrained in everything NCS does as a telecommunications equipment and applications provider. In fact, a specialized organization within NCS searches for efficiencies, assists with process improvements where appropriate, and helps NCS become more effective in responding to customers' needs.

One of North America's largest business communications companies for sales and service, NCS is strong—geographically, financially, and technologically. The superior Nortel products and applications that NCS provides will take its customers well into the next century. These are important points to consider when choosing the right partner for a business communications system.

NETWORK SOLUTIONS

No one offers Nortel's industry-renowned network solutions with the same outstanding service and engineering skill that NCS brings to every customer relationship. As the communications world continues changing, NCS remains committed to Nortel's mission: to provide network solutions that meet the needs of even the most sophisticated customers.

WITH THE NCS 2-HOUR SERVICE GUARANTEE, THE COMPANY GUARANTEES THAT, IN AN EMERGENCY, NCS WILL FIX THE PROBLEM REMOTELY, OR BE ON-SITE WORKING ON THE PROBLEM WITHIN TWO HOURS (LEFT).

NO ONE OFFERS NORTEL'S INDUSTRY-RENOWNED NETWORK SOLUTIONS WITH THE SAME OUTSTANDING SERVICE AND ENGINEERING SKILL THAT NCS BRINGS TO EVERY CUSTOMER RELATIONSHIP (RIGHT).

J&H Marsh & McLennan, Inc.

IN MARCH 1997, JOHNSON & HIGGINS AND MARSH & MCLENNAN, TWO giant commercial insurance brokerage firms that began doing business more than a century ago, announced that they were merging. The new company, known as J&H Marsh & McLennan, Inc., is by far the world's largest insurance/reinsurance broker and risk management consulting firm, with more than 25,000 professionals and more than 500 offices worldwide. This merger also united Foster Higgins and the Mercer Consulting Group, creating the world's largest employee benefit and human resources consulting firm.

Locally, J&H Marsh & McLennan and Mercer Consulting employ more than 325 professionals and manage in excess of $750 million in annual premiums. Both companies are consistently ranked by their competitors as the top firms in the business and enjoy a reputation of the highest caliber. The firm's quality service is demonstrated by a client retention rate that has exceeded 90 percent over a 10-year span.

With the exceptional talent of the local staff, as well as the ability to draw upon its experts around the world, J&H Marsh & McLennan has earned distinction locally, as well as throughout its global network. The local staff has been awarded the coveted Chairman's Cup (recognizing the number one ranked office in the United States) several times in recent years for its outstanding quantitative and qualitative performance.

Specialists

Being part of a firm with such a large international network gives J&H Marsh & McLennan a distinctive edge over its local competition. It's a tremendous plus for the firm to have highly skilled local expertise, as well as having access to resources around the globe.

Fortune 1000 companies historically had been the lifeblood of both Johnson & Higgins and Marsh & McLennan prior to and after the merger. Together, the two firms have had an outstanding rate of success serving the sophisticated risk management needs of these clients (14 of the 15 largest public companies in the area are clients at this writing). The challenge in continuing to grow was to bring its expertise and market clout to midsized companies without letting them become a "small fish in a big pond." The firm's solution was to form "a business within a business"—the Insurance Services Division (ISD). Its dedicated professionals have access to all of the company's global resources, but work exclusively with midsized companies. Today, ISD comprises one-third of the firm's business worldwide and more than 35 percent of its business in Washington.

To meet the needs of a wide variety of clients, J&H Marsh & McLennan has an extensive range of capabilities, including professionals specializing in environmental liability, directors and officers liability, professional liability, captive insurance company formation, and safety and loss control services, as well as risk management information systems and claims consulting. In addition, the firm's employees include specialists in surety bonding, international risk management consulting, property insurance, and health, medical, and disability insurance.

ON WORLDWIDE J&H DAY, EACH J&H OFFICE CLOSES FOR BUSINESS AND REDIRECTS STAFF TO HELP CHILDREN'S SCHOOLS, DAY CARE CENTERS, AND SUPPORT ORGANIZATIONS IN THEIR COMMUNITIES (LEFT).

WITH THE EXCEPTIONAL TALENT OF THE LOCAL STAFF, AS WELL AS THE ABILITY TO DRAW UPON ITS EXPERTS AROUND THE WORLD, J&H OF WASHINGTON HAS EARNED DISTINCTION LOCALLY, AS WELL AS THROUGHOUT THE J&H GLOBAL NETWORK (RIGHT).

J. BURKE LONG

DAVID HITTLE

DAVID HITTLE

CUTTING-EDGE TECHNOLOGY

In today's electronic age, J&H Marsh & McLennan has taken advantage of the latest technology to link its staff globally. Its proprietary network enables employees to connect with one another and to track important developments in the industries they serve. These professionals have immediate and simultaneous access to Securities and Exchange Commission documents on public companies and profiles of private companies.

The network is also tied to real-time news feeds from Knight-Ridder, Dow Jones, and PR Newswire, as well as the *Wall Street Journal* and other publications around the world. This information can be filtered and customized on each employee's desktop. The virtual team constructed through this network is able to work together to solve client problems, opening up resources worldwide.

J&H DAY

As part of its 150th anniversary observance in 1995, prior to the merger, J&H opted to give something back to the communities it serves by sponsoring a day to help children in

need around the world. Each office was closed for business on May 11, 1995, and staff were redirected to help children's schools, day care centers, and support organizations in their communities. This program was so well received by the firm's employees, the children, and the organizations that Worldwide J&H Day for children has become an annual event.

In Washington, requests for help stream in year-round. Beneficiaries of the corporate-sponsored event range from elementary schools to the Boys & Girls Club, from a children's hospital to an abuse shelter for women and children. J&H has attempted to fill as many of the requests as possible.

Some J&H employees have visited with patients at the Hospital for Sick Children. J&H painting, cleaning, and landscaping crews have reported for duty at Langdon Elementary School, the North Michigan Park and Recreation Center, the Teen Mothers' Center, and the House of Ruth. J&H employees even helped build a deck at the Learning Center.

All this hard work has its rewards. Along with a stream of requests for help, J&H employ-

ees have received praise and thanks for their efforts. The sense of accomplishment and appreciation has inspired employees to look forward to the next year's event with anticipation. According to Dick Duncan, president and branch manager of the D.C. office, "We believe this tradition will be maintained in the merged company as evidence that J&H Marsh & McLennan employees are not only professionals—they're also good citizens."

J&H MARSH & McLENNAN ON SUCCESS

The firm has enjoyed tremendous success in the Washington market. This success has been achieved by staying focused on two key principles: providing professional services that the firm's clients want and value, and attracting, developing, and retaining the very best professionals in the industry.

The firm is committed to staying focused on these guiding principles, to maintaining its technological leadership in its industry, and to continuing its support of the Washington community and all the communities where the firm does business around the world.

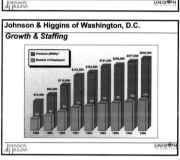

CLOCKWISE FROM TOP LEFT: J&H MARSH & MCLENNAN HAS LONG SERVED THE CONSTRUCTION INDUSTRY IN WASHINGTON, REPRESENTING MAJOR CONTRACTORS AS WELL AS DEVELOPING "WRAP-UP" INSURANCE PROGRAMS.

THE INFORMATION NETWORK ENABLES EMPLOYEES TO CONNECT WITH ONE ANOTHER AND TO TRACK IMPORTANT DEVELOPMENTS IN THE INDUSTRIES THEY SERVE.

J&H MARSH & MCLENNAN'S CLIENT RETENTION RATE OF MORE THAN 98 PERCENT AND ITS COMPOUNDED GROWTH RATE OF MORE THAN 25 PERCENT ARE UNPARALLELED.

PHOTOGRAPHERS

TIMOTHY BICKEL, a native of Indianapolis, works for Eastman Kodak Company. He specializes in wedding photos, portraiture, and stock photography. Bickel's images were featured in another Towery publication, *Louisville: A River Serenade*.

WENDY W. CORTESI, originally from New York, is a freelance natural science photographer who graduated from Wellesley College with a bachelor's degree in art history. A member of the Biological Photographers Association (BPA), she won the BPA Education Award in the 1993 Professional Exhibition and her work has been published in *BPA Journal*. In addition, Cortesi's images can be seen in *Country*, *Dominion*, and *National Geographic* magazines. She is the author of two books, *Explore a Spooky Swamp* and *White House Guide Book*, which was produced in conjunction with the National Geographic Society.

RICHARD DAY lives in Alma, Illinois, where he operates Daybreak Imagery. His areas of specialty include travel photography and outdoor images of all kinds, especially birds. Day's work has appeared in numerous national publications, including *Audubon*, *Ducks Unlimited*, *Field & Stream*, and *National Geographic Traveler*, as well as in various advertisements, calendars, and books.

WILLIAM B. FOLSOM, owner and operator of McLean, Virginia-based William B. Folsom Photography, Inc., has a stock photography file of more than 37,000 images on such subjects as the U.S. Armed Forces, aviation, high technology, and North American animals. In addition to more than 75 cover photographs for such publications as *Time*, *Civil War Times Illustrated*, Delta Air Lines' *Sky* magazine, and the *Washington Flyer*, Folsom has contributed to nearly 30 books,

including *Algonquians of the East Coast* (Time-Life Books) and *Smithsonian Guide to Aviation* (Macmillan Publishing).

HILLSTROM STOCK PHOTO, established in 1967, is a full-service stock photography agency. The Chicago-based agency's files include images of architecture, agriculture backgrounds, classic autos, gardens, and high-risk adventure/sports.

JIM KIRBY has worked as an advertising and editorial photographer for designers, corporations, and magazines since 1985. Specializing in photographs of people, including formal portraiture, he most enjoys capturing people in their environments. The winner of 10 Virginia Press Association awards for excellence in photography, Kirby is an active member of the American Society of Media Photographers (ASMP), and his clients include Mobil, IBM, Signet Bank, Special Olympics International, and Habitat for Humanity.

JAMES LEMASS studied art in his native Ireland before moving to Cambridge, Massachusetts, in 1987. His areas of specialty include people and travel photography, and his work can be seen in publications by Aer Lingus, British Airways, and USAir, and in the NYNEX Yellow Pages. Lemass has also worked for the Massachusetts Office of Travel and Tourism, and his photographs have appeared in two other Towery publications, *New York: Metropolis of the American Dream* and *Treasures on Tampa Bay: Tampa, St. Petersburg, Clearwater*.

ROBERT LLEWELLYN, a native of Roanoke, specializes in landscape, aerial, and architectural photography. Some 22 of his books have been published, one of which—*Washington, The Capital*—was

picked as an official diplomatic gift of the White House. Llewellyn is the recipient of numerous awards, including the Art Direction Creativity Award, the *Communications Arts* Annual Award, and awards from the art directors clubs of New York and Washington.

GREG PEASE is a Baltimore-based photographer specializing in corporate and industrial photography. Having begun his career as a commercial photographer in 1974, he has won numerous awards, and his images have been published in books, magazines, and advertisements worldwide. Best known for his regional landscape and maritime photography, Pease is coprincipal of Greg Pease & Associates with his wife, Kelly.

DANIELE PIASECKI, an award-winning photographer who hails from France, moved to the United States in 1992. Her love of travel led to her passion for photography, and her fine art photographs have been featured in more than 110 juried exhibitions, as well as in the prestigious Stephenson Calendar. Piasecki regards photography as "a way to bring beauty, serenity, peace, and light into other people's lives." Currently, she lives in Alexandria, Virginia.

LIZ ROLL, an Arlington, Virginia-based freelance photographer, worked as a photographer and lab technician for the American Red Cross National Headquarters in Washington from 1988 to 1992. Specializing in portrait, location, and public relations photography, she has captured on film several natural disasters, including the massive earthquake that leveled Kobe, Japan, in 1995. A native of Long Island, Roll graduated from the Rochester Institute of Technology in New York State with a bachelor of fine arts in photographic illustration.

MAE SCANLAN is a Washington, D.C.-based stock photographer who specializes in scenic, travel, nature, and animal photography. Her images have appeared nationally and internationally in books, calendars, and magazines, as well as in displays, posters, and videos. The book of Scanlan's images, called *Beautiful America's Washington, D.C.*, was recently published in its third edition.

RON SCHRAMM specializes in photographing architectural elements within the environment, as well as capturing his native Chicago on film. His images can be seen in numerous newspapers, brochures, exhibits, and advertising pieces; on wall murals and magazine covers; and in *Chicago: A Pictorial Guide*. A member of the ASMP, American Society of Picture Professionals, and Chicago Convention & Visitors Bureau, he owns Ron Schramm Photography, a stock agency with a comprehensive file of images.

JOHN SKOWRONSKI first picked up a camera at age 30, and photography soon consumed his life, taking the place of his computer programming career. The capital city was his first subject, and he continues to find unexpected ways to reveal Washington's familiar sights. Skowronski's areas of specialty are architectural and still life photography, as well as portraiture. His images are used by editorial, corporate, and advertising clients across North America.

ALEX WATERHOUSE-HAYWARD, a native of Buenos Aires, was a high school teacher in Mexico City 20 years ago when he moved with his wife and children to Vancouver, British Columbia. He has been an editorial photographer specializing in people ever since. Waterhouse-Hayward has freelanced for numerous Canadian magazines and is a regular contributor to the *Globe & Mail*. His work has appeared in *Interview*, *Time*, *People*, *Entertainment Weekly*, *Esquire*, *I-D*, *Arena*, *Spin*, *Vanity Fair*, *Future Sex*, and the *Los Angeles Times*.

Other photographers and organizations that contributed to *Washington: City on a Hill* include Paul Alers, Jocelyn Augustino, Karen Ballard, Ken Cedeno, Steve Crowley, Burt Goulait, John Harrington, Peter Harris, Mary E. Messenger, Cliff Owen, Kenny Pang, Mark Reinstein, Daniel Rosenbaum, the *Washington Times*, and Tracy Woodward.

INDEX OF PROFILES